LET THEM IN

LET THEM IN

THE CASE FOR
OPEN BORDERS

─────────── ★ ───────────

JASON L. RILEY

GOTHAM
BOOKS

GOTHAM BOOKS
Published by Penguin Group (USA) Inc.
375 Hudson Street, New York, New York 10014, U.S.A.
Penguin Group (Canada), 90 Eglinton Avenue East, Suite 700, Toronto, Ontario M4P 2Y3,
Canada (a division of Pearson Penguin Canada Inc.); Penguin Books Ltd, 80 Strand, London
WC2R 0RL, England; Penguin Ireland, 25 St Stephen's Green, Dublin 2, Ireland (a division
of Penguin Books Ltd); Penguin Group (Australia), 250 Camberwell Road, Camberwell,
Victoria 3124, Australia (a division of Pearson Australia Group Pty Ltd); Penguin Books
India Pvt Ltd, 11 Community Centre, Panchsheel Park, New Delhi – 110 017, India; Penguin
Group (NZ), 67 Apollo Drive, Rosedale, North Shore 0632, New Zealand (a division of
Pearson New Zealand Ltd); Penguin Books (South Africa) (Pty) Ltd, 24 Sturdee Avenue,
Rosebank, Johannesburg 2196, South Africa

Penguin Books Ltd, Registered Offices: 80 Strand, London WC2R 0RL, England

Published by Gotham Books, a member of Penguin Group (USA) Inc.

First printing, April 2008
10 9 8 7 6 5 4 3 2 1

Gotham Books and the skyscraper logo are trademarks of Penguin Group (USA) Inc.

LIBRARY OF CONGRESS CATALOGING-IN-PUBLICATION DATA

Riley, Jason.
    Let them in: the case for open borders / Jason L. Riley.—1st ed.
        p.   cm.
    Includes bibliographical references.
    ISBN 978-1-592-40349-3
    1. United States—Emigration and immigration—Government policy. 2. United
States—Emigration and immigration.   I. Title.
    JV6483.R55 2008
    325.73—dc22   2008006654

Printed in the United States of America
Set in Van Dijck with Sackers Gothic
Designed by Sabrina Bowers

FOR NAOMI

CONTENTS

———————————— ★ ————————————

America is really many Americas. We call ourselves a nation of immigrants, and that's truly what we are. We have drawn people from every corner of the Earth. We're composed of virtually every race and religion, and not in small numbers, but large. We have a statue in New York Harbor that speaks of this—a statue of a woman holding a torch of welcome to those who enter our country to become Americans. She has greeted millions upon millions of immigrants to our country. She welcomes them still. She represents our open door.

All of the immigrants who came to us brought their own music, literature, customs, and ideas. And the marvelous thing, a thing of which we're proud, is they did not have to relinquish these things in order to fit in. In fact, what they brought to America became American. And this diversity has more than enriched us; it has literally shaped us.—RONALD REAGAN

LET THEM IN

INTRODUCTION

---★---

The magazines and the illustrators are long gone and largely forgotten, but the images endure. Like the 1903 print from *Judge*, a popular political magazine of the period. It's titled, "The Immigrant: Is he an Acquisition or a Detriment?" and depicts a hulking, exhausted new arrival to America's shores. He wears ragged clothing and lumbers inland with his wife, all their possessions in tow. As human cargo ships sail to and fro in the distance, a small mob greets the man, each individual representing a voice in the raucous turn-of-the-century immigration debate. A contractor says, "He gives me cheap labor." A workman says, "He cheapens my labor." A health officer says, "He brings disease." A citizen calls him "a menace." A politician says, "He makes votes for me." Silently determined, the man stares straight ahead, ignoring them all.

Sound familiar?

The targets have changed in the past century, but the concerns have not. Today, we're still being told that when immigrants aren't busy depressing wages; displacing workers; and overrunning our schools, hospitals, and jails, they're compromising our national security. But attacks that were once directed at Asians and Europeans—along with Catholics and Jews—are now directed primarily at Mexicans and other Latin Americans who in recent decades have comprised the bulk of newcomers. Steve King, a congressman from Iowa, compares Mexican aliens to livestock. Tom Tancredo, a Colorado congressman who sports T-shirts announcing that AMERICA IS FULL, says Hispanic immigrants have turned Miami into "a Third World country." And Don Goldwater, nephew of conservative icon Barry Goldwater and an unsuccessful candidate for governor in Arizona, has called for interring illegal immigrants in concentration camps and pressing them into forced labor building a wall across the southern U.S. border.

Playing on post-9/11 fears, political candidates in California have distributed flyers depicting Mexican immigrants as turbaned Islamic terrorists. Volunteer border patrol groups like the Minuteman Project insist that migrants sneaking across the Sonoran Desert aren't just coming here to work and feed their families but also to "reconquer" the Southwest. And despite the fact that, relative to natives, the undocumented are more likely to have jobs and less likely to engage in crime, Newt Gingrich maintains that "young Americans in our cities are [being] massacred" by illegal aliens and says the "war here at home" against these immigrants is "even more deadly than the war in Iraq and Afghanistan."

Cable news personalities like Lou Dobbs tell us that Salvadorans, Guatemalans, and other Latino migrants bear infectious diseases that imperil U.S. citizens and leave our health-care system teetering on bankruptcy. Talk radio hosts like Michael Savage have urged Americans to protest the presence of Latinos by burning the Mexican flag. J. D. Hayworth, a former Arizona congressman who became a talk radio host after losing his seat in 2006, says we should give America's estimated 12 million undocumented residents—half of whom have been here more than five years and many of whom have married American citizens and borne American children—120 days to leave the country voluntarily and then deport the remainders by force. Mike Huckabee, a 2008 Republican presidential hopeful and former governor of Arkansas, adopted Hayworth's idea as part of his official campaign platform. Huckabee's reward was an endorsement from Jim Gilchrist, the founder of the Minuteman Project.

Nativists warn that the brown influx from Mexico is soiling our Anglo-American cultural fabric, damaging our social mores, and facilitating a U.S. identity crisis. Anti-immigrant screeds with hysterical titles like *Invasion* by Michelle Malkin and *State of Emergency* by Pat Buchanan have become best-sellers. Tomes by serious academics like Samuel Huntington and Victor Davis Hanson make the same arguments using bigger words and giving the cruder polemicists some intellectual cover.

And then there's the odd bed-sharing. Liberal columnists like Nicholas Kristof of *The New York Times* and conservative policy analysts like Robert Rector of The Heritage Foundation both fret that immigration from Mexico merely swells the ranks of the U.S. poor and burdens our social services. Republicans convinced that Mexican immigrants are natural Democrats find common cause with both the economic protectionists, who say immigrants crib jobs, and the population-control environmentalists, who want the border sealed on grounds that the United States already has too many people.

All of them, however, arrive at the same pessimistic conclusion, which is that immigration on balance is a net negative for the United States. They go to great lengths to demonstrate that today's new arrivals are different from yesterday's, that those coming from Latin America are sui generis, uniquely incapable of assimilation. They cite special circumstances that made the past acculturation of European and Asian immigration possible but render it impossible for Latinos. They view these foreigners as a liability rather than an asset. They want an immigration "time-out."

What Would Reagan Do?

If you're a free-market conservative in the Ronald Reagan tradition, this debate has been doubly depressing because so much of the bellyaching has originated with the political right, where many people have convinced themselves that scapegoating immigrants for America's economic and social ills—real and imagined—is a winner at the polls. On the topic of immigration, at least, too many conservatives have pocketed their principles and morphed into reactionary Populists. They claim to be Reaganites, but temperamentally and rhetorically they have more in common with Pat Buchanan, if not Father Coughlin. Their right-wing version of the "angry left" promotes a politics of resentment, frustration, and fear. It stirs up isolationism and xenophobia. And as a political strategy it's heretofore been a loser, just like Buchanan in his presidential bids.

Besides, the nativist noise that has saturated so much of talk radio, cable news, and conservative print journalism in recent years is about as far from the Gipper's style as you can get. To Reagan, ever the optimist, America was "a shining city upon a Hill," in the John Winthrop phrase that he liked to use. Liberal immigration policies were proof that this country remained a land of opportunity, a nation built on the idea of liberty, not the *Blut und Boden* European doctrine.

Reagan held this view long before he became president, as Lou Cannon, his biographer, has documented. In 1952, when the United States was still under the thumb of highly restrictive immigration quotas enacted in the 1920s, Reagan gave a speech endorsing open borders. In his view, America was "the promised land" for people from "any place in the world." Reagan said "any person with the courage, with the desire to tear up their roots, to strive for freedom, to attempt and dare to live in a strange land and foreign place, to travel halfway across the world was welcome here."

In a 1977 radio address, Reagan discussed what he called "the illegal alien fuss. Are great numbers of our unemployed really victims of the illegal alien invasion, or are those illegal tourists actually doing work our own people won't do? One thing is certain in this hungry world: No regulation or law should be allowed if it results in crops rotting in the fields for lack of harvesters." The next time you tune into Rush Limbaugh, Sean Hannity, Laura Ingraham, Hugh Hewitt, and Dennis Prager, contrast their take on immigration with radio Reagan's.

Reagan understood that immigrants are coming here to work, not live on the dole. He also grasped that natives and immigrants don't compete with one another for jobs in a zero-sum labor market and that our policy makers would do better to focus less on protecting U.S. workers from immigrant competition and more on expanding the economic pie. In his November 1979 speech announcing his candidacy for president, Reagan called for free labor flows throughout

North America. Reagan knew that immigration, like free trade, which he also supported, benefits everyone in the long run.

Later in the campaign, in December 1979, Reagan responded to criticism from conservative columnist Holmes Alexander. "Please believe me when I tell you the idea of a North American accord has been mine for many, many years," said the future president. And conservatives calling today for a wall along the entire United States–Mexico border should know that Reagan was not a big fan of that prospect. "Some months before I declared," he continued in his response to Alexander, "I asked for a meeting and crossed the border to meet with the president of Mexico. . . . I went, as I said in my announcement address, to ask him his ideas— how we could make the border something other than a locale for a nine-foot fence."

At the end of his presidency, Reagan was still invoking Winthrop. "I've spoken of the shining city all my political life, but I don't know if I ever quite communicated what I saw when I said it," he remarked in his 1989 farewell address to the nation. "But in my mind it was a tall proud city built on rocks stronger than oceans, wind-swept, God-blessed, and teeming with people of all kinds living in harmony and peace, a city with free ports that hummed with commerce and creativity, and if there had to be city walls, the walls had doors and the doors were open to anyone with the will and the heart to get here."

It's true that in 1986 Reagan signed the Immigration Control and Reform Act, which included employer sanctions and more border security, but he also insisted on a provision for legalizing immigrants already in the United States. Which is to say, he supported "amnesty." In his signing statement, he said, "We have consistently supported a legalization program which is both generous to the alien and fair to the countless thousands of people throughout the world who seek legally to come to America. The legalization provisions in this act will go far to improve the lives of a class of individuals who now must hide in the shadows, without access to many of the benefits of a free and open society. Very soon many of these men and women will be able to step into the sunlight and, ultimately, if they choose, they may become Americans."

SAME OLD, SAME OLD

Most every anti-immigrant argument rolled out today is a retread. Benjamin Franklin was complaining about bilingual sign posts and "swarms" of unassimilable Germans migrating to Pennsylvania 250 years ago. Later, in the nineteenth century, people like Samuel Morse, inventor of the telegraph and a leading nativist of his day, would pick up Franklin's banner. Morse was a founder and generous financier of the anti-immigrant and anti-Catholic Know-Nothing movement, and in lieu of Germans he railed against Irish immigration in the antebellum decades. In his 1835 treatise against the political influence of Catholicism, Morse argued that poor, uneducated Irish Catholics were subverting the values and ideals of Anglo-America and should therefore be kept out of the country.

Opposition to Asian immigration came next. By the latter part of the nineteenth century, "Yellow Peril" was all the rage, stoked by increased Chinese migration to the American West. A famous 1881 illustration first published in *The Wasp*, a San Francisco–based literary magazine edited by Ambrose Bierce, depicts Lady Liberty as a Chinese coolie gripping an opium pipe. The rays of light emanating from the statue's head are labeled "Immorality," "Filth," "Disease," and "Ruin to White Labor."

Henry George, who would later become an influential political economist, first gained prominence denouncing what he called the "Mongolization of America." In 1881, George wrote of "the supreme law of self-preservation which justifies us in shutting out a non-assimilable element fraught for us with great social and political dangers." He warned that Asians "will introduce into the life of the republic race prejudices and social bitterness." He said they would "reduce wages and degrade labor, and widen the gulf between rich and poor." And like today's nativists, George was concerned that "the Chinese, if free play be allowed their immigration, [will] supplant the white race."

SLOUCHING TOWARD GUATEMALA?

Modern-day restrictionists either don't know this history or are hoping the public doesn't know it. But what's most relevant about these time-honored arguments is that those spouting them have a perfect record of being wrong. Immigration alarmism sells books and boosts TV and radio ratings, but its doomsday scenarios never seem to come to fruition.

Elite thinkers today continue to insist that U.S. culture is slouching toward Guatemala. In his 2004 book *Who Are We?* Harvard political scientist Samuel Huntington writes that "contemporary immigration is unprecedented in American history" and that "the experience and lessons of past immigration have little relevance to understanding its dynamics and consequences." As far as Huntington is concerned, the historical record should have little bearing on immigration public policy decisions going forward. Curious notion, that.

The immigration issue is the fool's gold of American politics. Voters like to sound off to pollsters about it, yet they inevitably pull the lever on Election Day with other matters foremost in mind. Elections seldom if ever turn on immigration, and the GOP restrictionist message so adored by talk radio, cable news, and the blogosphere once again failed to deliver the goods in 2006, when Republicans lost control of the House and Senate.

Worse, the GOP had made "securing the border" a loud national theme in the run-up to the 2006 election, only to do nothing about it save for approving a few hundred miles of fence along a two-thousand-mile border. Republicans thus managed to highlight either their fecklessness in failing to do something about an allegedly urgent problem or their cynicism in raising the issue at all.

The GOP has a long history of fumbling immigration. And President George W. Bush, a former border-state governor who knows the issue well, has tried to steer conservatism and Republicanism away from repeating those mistakes with Hispanics, who are the country's fastest-growing voting bloc. Mr. Bush doesn't want his party to lose Latinos the way its xenophobic message in the early twentieth century turned away Irish, Italian, and Asian voters for decades.

But this isn't just about identity politics, which conservatives by and large are happy to leave to the political left. It's also about America playing to its strengths. Like Reagan before him, Bush understands that immigrants help the United States stay atop the global marketplace. A liberal immigration policy has served the country quite well over the past two centuries, and the numbers coming today are hardly extraordinary. Since the government began keeping count in 1820, the United States has absorbed a world-leading 60 million immigrants from some 170 nations. The latest census data puts our foreign-born population at 33.5 million, which is roughly the population of Canada. In terms of absolute numbers, that's a record. But as a percentage of the total U.S. population, it's still well below the historic highs reached in 1890 and 1910.

Immigrants prefer America because it remains the world's foremost tribune to freedom and opportunity. Its magnetism is a testament to the country's global standing. Even better, it's an indication that America is still winning the international battle for talent and human capital that will keep it competitive for generations to come.

RICHER AND SAFER

This book expounds on two general themes. The first is that, contrary to received wisdom, today's Latino immigrants aren't "different," just newer. The second is that an open immigration policy is compatible with free-market conservatism and homeland security. I explain, from a conservative perspective, why the pessimists who say otherwise are mistaken. I argue that immigrants, including low-skill immigrants, are an asset to the United States, not a liability. Immigrants help keep our workforce younger and stronger than Asia's and Europe's. As entrepreneurs, they create jobs. As consumers, they generate economic activity that results in more overall economic growth. By taking jobs that overqualified Americans spurn, they fill niches in the workforce that make our economy more efficient and allow for the upward mobility of the native population.

An immigration policy that acknowledges these economic realities would provide more, not fewer, legal ways for immigrants to enter the country. That, in turn, would go a long way toward reducing illegal entries. It would also alleviate pressure on the border and free up our overburdened patrols to track down terrorists, drug dealers, and other serious threats to our welfare. Unfortunately, as things stand, our border security officers spend most of their time chasing migrants who come north to mow our lawns and burp our babies. A guest-worker program for such individuals would help regulate the labor flow and isolate the criminals, thus making us much safer than any wall along the Rio Grande.

———————— ★ ————————

CHAPTER ONE

POPULATION:
DOOM AND DEMOGRAPHY

*Perhaps this is the first instance in which those with
their pants up are going to be caught by those with
their pants down!*—JOHN TANTON

Odd political bedfellows are nothing new in the nation's
capital, but a House Judiciary Subcommittee hearing held
on March 24, 2004, was remarkable all the same. The witnesses invited to testify that day included Roy Beck, Mark
Krikorian, and Frank Morris. All three worked for organizations set up in the 1980s and '90s by John Tanton, a radical
environmentalist and staunch supporter of Planned Parenthood. Morris was also a former director of the Congressional
Black Caucus Foundation, and, at the time, he was actively
campaigning for a slot on the board of the nation's leading
green group, the Sierra Club.

Despite their liberal credentials, however, the trio

wasn't appearing at the behest of Democrats. They were there at the urging of the subcommittee's Republican chairman, John Hostettler of Indiana, one of Congress's foremost social conservatives. A Baptist from Evansville who's since left office, Hostettler had first been elected in 1994 with crucial backing from pro-life groups, along the way even earning the moniker "McGingrich" from one of his political opponents. And the environmentalists hated him almost as much as the abortion-rights activists. Hostettler had voted to allow oil drilling in Alaska's Arctic National Wildlife Refuge, and in 2004 he earned a rating of nine out of one hundred—among the lowest in Congress—from the League of Conservation Voters, which gauges lawmakers' earth friendliness based on key votes concerning energy, natural resources, and the environment.

But none of that mattered for the purposes of the hearing. That's because the topic was immigration, and any political differences between Hostettler and his witnesses were trumped by their shared belief that today's newcomers harm America. Anti-immigrant sentiment coming from the political right tends to dominate the headlines, but the environmental left has always played a central role in efforts to tighten the U.S. border. For restrictionist greens, though, the main issue isn't the economy or even homeland security. It's the human species—more specifically, human population growth. The environmentalists want fewer people on the planet because they believe that additional human beings will have a negative effect on the supply of land, food, and other extractive resources. And they want fewer people migrating here for the same reason. The greater the population, they argue, the bigger the threat to nature.

Sierra Club Secessionists

One survey of twenty leading U.S. environmental organizations found fourteen that consider overpopulation to be "a problem." The Environmental Defense Fund's Population Statement says that "resolv[ing] the world's major environmental challenges will require stabilizing the world's population at the lowest possible level." The National Audubon Society says it "focuses on supporting U.S. family planning assistance programs in order to reduce fertility in developing nations and in the U.S." According to the "Population Policy" of the Wilderness Society, "To bring population levels to ecologically sustainable levels, both birth rates and immigration rates need to be reduced."

"Stabilizing world population" ranks fourth on the Sierra Club's twenty-first-century to-do list, but that's not high enough for some. And it so happens that right around the time of the Hostettler hearing, a large bloc of anti-immigrant Sierrans were attempting a coup. It had been the second such attempt in recent years. For decades the club, which was cofounded in 1892 by a Scottish immigrant named John Muir, had agitated for less immigration to the United States as a way of limiting population growth. Back in 1968, it had even copublished Paul Ehrlich's antinatal bestseller, *The Population Bomb.* By the mid-1990s, however, it had piped down the restrictionist rhetoric. Immigration had become an especially contentious issue due to Proposition 187, a 1994 ballot initiative in California that denied public education and health care to illegal aliens. And in 1996, the San Francisco–based Sierra Club announced it would no longer take a position on immigration levels.

Partly, this had to do with a mostly white and entirely elitist organization fearing charges of racism. And then there was the more practical matter of fund-raising. A *Los Angeles Times* article later revealed that the Sierra Club's largest individual donor was a retired hedge fund manager named David Gelbaum who'd quietly given more that $100 million to the organization. A descendent of Ukrainian Jewish immigrants who was married to a Mexican American, Gelbaum told the paper, "I cannot support an organization that is anti-immigration. It would dishonor the memory of my grandparents." He added that in the mid-nineties he had informed Carl Pope, who would later become the club's executive director, that "if they ever came out anti-immigration, they would never get a dollar from me."

In any case, the club's new, pseudo-agnostic stand on

immigration angered so many members that a referendum was held two years later on whether or not to call for a "reduction in net immigration." The proposal was defeated, 60–40, but proponents, who maintained that population growth was "the most fundamental issue" for the green movement, were undeterred. They began in earnest to recruit anti-immigrant figures to sit on the Sierra Club's fifteen-member board of directors. And by 2004 that rebel faction of the club was poised to take the reins and yank them in a decidedly restrictionist direction. It had already elected five sympathetic board members in the past two elections. Sierrans would vote to fill five more seats on the panel in April of that year, and the activists were pushing three of their hand-picked candidates—former Colorado governor Richard Lamm, Cornell professor David Pimentel, and Frank Morris.

The club's leadership was so worried about these dissident challengers that in the run-up to the election it sent out ballot notices to members, warning them about outsiders trying to "take over" the organization. Past leaders of the group also phoned and e-mailed members and asked them to vote for candidates selected by the club's nominating committee, all of whom advocated a neutral stand on immigration.

It worked.

The anti-immigrant slate was defeated, and the leadership's candidates won all five seats in the largest turnout ever for a club election.

THE PUPPETEER

For immigrant restrictionists, the battle may have been lost but the war continues. And that's thanks in no small part to the efforts of one man, John Tanton. Tanton and his organizations were working in the shadows for years to foment the Sierra Club upheaval. ("The Sierra Club may not want to touch the immigration issue, but the immigration issue is going to touch the Sierra Club," he once vowed.) And Tanton-linked groups and individuals have played major roles in drumming up faux grassroots anti-immigration sentiment nationwide. The head of one of Tanton's major organs, the Federation for American Immigration Reform (FAIR), claims to have testified before Congress more than fifty times. Tanton's extensive network shows how activists from across the political spectrum and with different agendas—population control, abortion rights, economic protectionism, racial purity—have coalesced around the issue of restricting immigration.

The three Republican witnesses who appeared at the Hostettler hearing all had direct ties to Tanton. Mark Krikorian, a veteran of FAIR, now runs the Center for Immigration Studies, an anti-immigrant FAIR spin-off founded by Tanton in 1985. Roy Beck heads NumbersUSA, a zero-population-growth (zpg) outfit set up by Tanton in 1996. Frank Morris is chairman of Choose Black America, another FAIR front-group set up in 2006 to convince black natives that immigrants are especially keen on stealing *their* jobs. And like Richard Lamm, his fellow collaborator in the failed Sierra Club putsch, Morris is a member of FAIR's board of advisors.

Tanton's voice isn't as readily identifiable as some others' singing from the anti-immigrant hymnal. Commentators like Pat Buchanan and Lou Dobbs, academics like Sam Huntington and Victor Davis Hanson, and politicians like Tom Tancredo and Lamar Smith are all better-known figures. Yet a 2006 profile of Tanton in *The Washington Post* referred to him as the "mastermind of the modern-day movement to curb immigration." That's not an overstatement. And research conducted by the Southern Poverty Law Center, a civil rights group, shows why.

Tanton is a retired ophthalmologist who lives in the tiny northern Michigan town of Petoskey (population 6,000), which is about as far from the front lines of the immigration brouhaha as you can get. A longtime environmentalist and member of the Sierra Club and Audubon Society, he turned his attention to population control in the 1960s after becoming familiar with the works of antinatal zealots like Paul Ehrlich and the late ecologist Garrett Hardin. If you think *zealot* is too strong a word, know that Ehrlich has said all U.S. aid to developing nations should be conditioned on the sterilization of Third World fathers with more than two children. And Hardin once asserted that "the freedom to breed will bring ruin to all." Hardin also believed that "either there must be a relatively painless weeding out before birth or a more painful and wasteful elimination of individuals after birth."

Tanton and his wife organized one of Michigan's first Planned Parenthood associations in 1965. By the mid-seventies he was the national president of Zero Population Growth. And in 1979, convinced that immigrants were to blame for overpopulation, which in turn would result in nature's doom, he founded FAIR.

Over the past four decades, Tanton has birthed or bank-rolled a loose-knit network of anti-immigrant and antinatal groups that continue to impact the national debate. In addition to FAIR, the Center for Immigration Studies, and NumbersUSA, it includes the American Immigration Control Foundation, Californians for Population Stabilization, and ProjectUSA. According to the Southern Poverty Law Center (SPLC), which labeled him "the Puppeteer" of the restrictionist movement, the "vast majority of American anti-immigration groups—more than a dozen in all—were either formed, led, or in other ways made possible through Tanton's efforts."

And if you're wondering why SPLC, a civil rights organization that specializes in tracking "hate groups," has Tanton on its radar screen, it's because the good doctor is also in cahoots with individuals and organizations that preach white supremacy. FAIR, by Tanton's own reckoning, has received some $1.5 million from the Pioneer Fund, a group dedicated to racial purity through eugenics. In the 1980s Tanton hosted retreats to discuss U.S. immigration policy, and attendees included open racists like Jared Taylor of the New Century Foundation. Taylor holds conferences attended by the likes of Klansman David Duke and edits a newsletter, *American Renaissance*, that's very popular with the white nationalist set. Tanton also wrote memos to attendees that betrayed a racialist agenda. In one that was later leaked to the press, Tanton said, "As Whites see their power and control over their lives declining, will they simply go quietly into the night?" And complaining about high Latino birth rates, he wrote, "Perhaps, this is the first instance in which those with their pants up are going to get caught by those with their pants down!"

Tanton doesn't merely hobnob with racists. He employs them and actively promotes their views. The Tanton network's publishing arm is The Social Contract Press, which publishes and distributes the works of all manner of unsavory characters. Among the more notable contributors is Peter Brimelow, a politically conservative anti-immigration immigrant from Britain who runs the white nationalist Web site, VDARE. Another favorite was the late Sam Francis, a VDARE writer and conservative columnist who was sacked by the *Washington Times* after giving a speech (at an American Renaissance conference) describing how the white race is bestowed with superior genes.

The editor of Social Contract Press, founded by Tanton in 1990, is Wayne Lutton, another ardent white nationalist. Lutton is a trustee at Jared Taylor's New Century Foundation and speaks at American Renaissance events. He sits on the advisory board of the Council of Conservative Citizens, the successor group to the White Citizens' Council that fought desegregation in the 1950s and 1960s. Pseudonymously, Lutton writes articles for *The Journal of Historical Review*, the in-house publication of the Holocaust-denying Institute for Historical Review. In 1994, he and Tanton coauthored a book titled *The Immigration Invasion*.

When I travel the country to report on immigration, or speak to groups in the know about Tanton and his network, I'm often asked why the mainstream media continue to cite groups like FAIR and the Center for Immigration Studies (CIS) without mentioning their origins or ulterior motives. CIS "reports" are given the gravitas of the Brookings Institution's, and FAIR is described as an organization that merely favors less immigration, when in fact its stated goal is to cut the U.S. population in half.

My reply is that in most cases it should be chalked up to ignorance (or laziness) rather than malice. The space constraints and daily deadlines of newspaper journalism often lend themselves to only so much exposition. But it's a credit to Tanton's tenaciousness that his "puppets"—folks like Dan Stein, Roy Beck, and Mark Krikorian—are considered by the press (and lawmakers) to be legitimate policy analysts making good-faith restrictionist arguments. Krikorian has written for the highly regarded Jewish neoconservative magazine *Commentary* and even managed to ingratiate himself with select movement conservatives. He writes regularly for *National Review*, which happens to count a fair number of devout Catholics among its editors. If there's one thing that bugs Tanton more than all those dusky people crossing the Rio Grande and overpopulating his country, it's that too many of them are Catholic, or so he once told the Associated Press.

RISE OF THE SOCIAL DARWINISTS

At first blush it might seem odd that one of the country's leading anti-immigration figures isn't a fire-breathing right-wing conservative but a tree hugger obsessed with population control. That someone like Tanton would also dabble in eugenics might seem stranger still. Historically speaking, however, those dots aren't difficult to connect. And in order to understand the contemporary immigration debate, it's important that these connections be drawn.

The origins of today's population control movement date to the nineteenth century and the Social Darwinist thinking that grew to florescence under the banner of eugenics, or improving the human race through controlled selective breeding. Under this theory of racial hygiene, some—not only some people but some peoples—are more "fit" than others. And the way to improve the lot of humanity was to encourage the propagation of the fit while mitigating or suppressing the propagation of the unfit.

This thinking later reached its apogee in Germany in the 1930s and 1940s, but it's popularity in America predated the Nazis and in some ways even inspired them. In 1907, Indiana became the first state to enact a sterilization law. California, Connecticut, Washington, and others soon followed. The Supreme Court blessed the medical procedure in a 1927 decision, *Buck v. Bell*, the one where Justice Oliver Wendell Holmes declared, "society can prevent those who are manifestly unfit from continuing their kind. . . . Three generations of imbeciles are enough." And though public opinion turned against them following World War II, sterilization programs survived in some states well into the 1960s, and in mental hospitals as late as the 1970s. In the end more than sixty-five thousand people in thirty-three states underwent forced sterilizations.

One of the country's leading eugenicists at the time was Harry Laughlin, who pushed (unsuccessfully) for a federal sterilization law. Laughlin also provided extensive testimony to Congress in support of the Immigration Act of 1924. The legislation was the brainchild of Albert Johnson, a senator from Washington State and honorary president of the Eugenics Research Association. It targeted the Italian and Russian (read: Jewish) influx of the early 1900s by limiting the number of immigrants who could be admitted from any country to 2 percent of the number of people from that country who were already present in the United States. Worried that these foreign hordes were diluting our "native stock," Laughlin told lawmakers that according to his research, an "excessive" number of immigrants coming from Southern and Eastern Europe were mentally deficient and thus "unfit."

Laughlin eventually became the House of Representative's chief eugenics advisor. In that capacity he drew up legislation that never became law in the United States but did provide the model for the Law for Prevention of Hereditarily Diseased Offspring, a compulsory sterilization measure enacted by Nazi Germany in 1933. Laughlin would go on to receive an honorary degree from the University of Heidelberg in 1936 for his work on the "science of racial cleansing." He also cofounded and was the first president of the Pioneer Fund, which would later serve as a major benefactor to John Tanton.

I don't know what Harry Laughlin thought about the environment. But I do know what the leading environmentalists of his day thought about eugenics and immigration. The word *eugenics* comes from the Greek term meaning "well-born" and was coined in 1883 by British hereditarian Sir Francis Galton, a cousin and confidante of Charles Darwin. (Both men, in fact, were fans of selective human breeding. Recall that the subtitle of Darwin's *On the Origin of Species by Means of Natural Selection* is *The Preservation of Favored Races in the Struggle for Life*.) The first international Congress of Eugenics was held in London in 1912. The second gathering was held in New York in 1921. It was hosted by the American Museum of Natural History at the urging of Henry Fairfield Osborn, the museum's president. A zoologist by training (and a nephew of J. P. Morgan), Osborn was the nation's pre-eminent naturalist and an intimate of Sierra Club founder John Muir. He was so enamored with eugenics that he had established the Galton Society at the museum in 1918. It joined the American Breeders Association, the Race Betterment Foundation, and other eugenics organizations that argued for stricter immigration controls to ward off racial suicide and preserve the environment. In his opening address to the conference, Osborn called for an immigration quota system and said eugenics should be the vehicle for promoting natural conservation in the United States.

The Galton Society was cofounded by Madison Grant, who's largely known for writing *The Passing of the Great Race*, a best-selling nativist polemic arguing that nonwhite immigrants—which included Southern and Eastern Europeans, according to his definition—were overpopulating America and corrupting the country's superior Nordic stock. "The immigrant laborers," he wrote, "are now breeding out their masters and killing by filth and by crowding as effectively as by sword." Grant was a lawyer with no background in history or science, but Osborn wrote the introduction to the book, lending credence—and the museum's stamp of approval—to wild assertions based on nothing more than racist dogma.

Grant was first and foremost an avid conservationist. He was head of the New York Zoological Society, a cofounder of the Bronx Zoo, and a pioneer of wildlife management who started and supported numerous environmental organizations throughout his lifetime. In a *New Yorker* magazine profile of the anthropologist Franz Boas, an opponent of eugenics and nemesis of Grant and Osborn, Grant is described as someone who'd "extended a passion for preserving bison and caribou into a mania for preserving the 'Nordic race.'"

John Tanton would understand.

PEOPLE ARE POLLUTION

Not all early proponents of eugenics were reactionary bigots. Many prominent progressive and socialist reformers also cottoned to the idea, reasoning that eugenics would help temper evil, unwieldy free-market capitalism and lead to more egalitarian socioeconomic outcomes. Europeans in this camp included Bertrand Russell, H. G. Wells, and George Bernard Shaw. And U.S. advocates included not only Justice Holmes but also Margaret Sanger, the birth control advocate who wanted "more children from the fit, less from the unfit." The founder of Planned Parenthood, Sanger is celebrated today as a feminist icon, but she was also a strong supporter of the 1924 immigration law, calling Eastern Europeans a "menace" to civilization. "While I personally believe in the sterilization of the feeble-minded, the insane, and the syphiletic," she wrote in 1919, "I have not been able to discover that these measures are more than superficial deterrents when applied to the constantly growing stream of the unfit. . . . Birth control, on the other hand, not only opens the way to the eugenist, but it preserves his work."

Nicholas Eberstadt, a demographer at the American Enterprise Institute who's written extensively about population control, says "the Hitler branch of eugenics was completely discredited, but the Sanger branch was not. And the Sanger branch gets us to today's zero population growth movement."

The "people are pollution" crowd often cites the eighteenth-century classical liberal economist Thomas Robert Malthus as their muse. But, just as John Maynard Keynes ultimately disowned what's referred to today as "Keynesian economics," Malthus, in the end, was no Malthusian. Which is to say that he was not immune to facts. And those invoking his name to buttress their antinatal arguments are distorting his population theory by ignoring the evolution of his arguments.

In 1798, at age thirty-two, Malthus published (anonymously) *An Essay on the Principle of Population*, in which he stated that "the power of population is indefinitely greater than the power of the earth to produce sustenance for man."

He further explained: "Population, when unchecked, increases in geometric ratio. Subsistence increases only in arithmetical ratio. A slight acquaintance with the numbers will show the immensity of the first power in comparison to the second."

Malthus's limits theories were wrong, as contemporary economic giants like David Ricardo did not hesitate to tell him, and as Malthus himself acknowledged in later editions of his initial essay. During his own lifetime, his prediction that more people would tend to produce a drop in the standard of living was proved false. Population and living standards rose simultaneously, and continue to do so today. Malthus would later say that he overstated his case. He conceded that all sorts of things can postpone or prevent the collision of human numbers and resources, including technological progress and what he called "moral restraint," or the rational decision by people to have fewer children.

Malthus's views adjusted over time as he looked at his "diminishing returns" model in more detail. In the second edition he wrote, "I have endeavored to soften some of the harshest conclusions of the first Essay." And in his conclusion to the fifth edition, he said:

From a review of the state of society in former periods, compared with the present, I should certainly say that the evils resulting from the principle of population have rather diminished than increased . . .

[and] it does not seem unreasonable to expect that they will be still further diminished. . . .

He continued:

On the whole, therefore, though our future prospects respecting the mitigation of the evils arising from the principle of population may not be so bright as we could wish, yet they are far from being entirely disheartening, and by no means preclude a gradual and progressive improvement in human society. . . . To the laws of property and marriage, and to the apparently narrow principle of self-interest which prompts each individual to exert himself in bettering his condition, we are indebted for all the noblest exertions of human genius.

Many popular and professional writers today "rely on the first edition's conclusions as being the essential Malthus," said the late economist Julian Simon, but "Malthus himself was a powerful critic of 'Malthusianism.' " Even Malthus biographer William Petersen noted, "From the first to the seventh edition of *An Essay on the Principle of Population,* its author moved from an ecological to a sociological perspective . . . and—most remarkably—from an unrelenting pessimism to a cautious optimism."

It wouldn't be a stretch to describe neo-Malthusians as the opposite of cautious and optimistic. Paul Ehrlich, their demigod, opened his 1968 book, *The Population Bomb*, with these words: "The battle to feed humanity is over. In the 1970s and 1980s hundreds of millions of people will starve to death in spite of any crash programs embarked upon now." In 1967, Lester Brown, another leading green who later founded the Worldwatch Institute, said, "The trend in grain stocks indicates clearly that 1961 marked a worldwide turning point. . . . [F]ood consumption moved ahead of food production." In his 2000 bestseller, *Earth in the Balance*, former vice president Al Gore insisted that "population is pushing many countries over an economic cliff as their resources are stripped away and the cycle of poverty and environmental destruction accelerates."

What's regrettable is that the views of these environmental ideologues haven't remained on the intellectual fringe, where they belong. Instead, they've guided the thinking of governments, international organizations, the press, and large swaths of an unwitting public. The notion that population growth causes or exacerbates poverty, resource scarcity, and ecological carnage has become received wisdom. In 1972 the Club of Rome, an influential global think tank, issued its "Limits to Growth" study, where it warned that the pace of population growth would lead directly to severe shortages of food, energy, minerals, trees, and other resources.

In 1980, the Carter administration issued the "Global 2000 Report," which stated: "If present trends continue, the world in 2000 will be more crowded, more polluted, less stable ecologically, and more vulnerable to disruption than the world we live in now. Serious stresses involving population, resources, and environment are clearly visible ahead. Despite greater material output, the world's people will be poorer in many ways than they are today." A 1994 World Population Conference report, signed by delegates from more than a hundred nations, called for "a sustainable balance between human numbers and the resources of the planet." And so on. Over the decades, the U.S. Department of Agriculture, the State Department, U.S. Aid for International Development, the World Bank, the United Nations, the Rockefeller Foundation, the Ford Foundation, and the MacArthur Foundation, among others, have forecasted fertility-related doom.

In most cases, enough time has passed to prove empirically that these predictions were spectacularly wrong. But then, facts and evidence don't really matter much to entrenched population alarmists. They are unwilling to test their hypotheses against data and reject them if they prove to be false. That's because hard-core environmentalism is much more of a secular theology than a reality-based, empirically sensitive approach to the world. And the essence of a faith is that your confidence in a proposition is not shaken by any factual disproof of given tests.

"For the socialist eugenicists and population controllers of the 1960s," Eberstadt tells me, "the proof of the righteousness of their viewpoint seemed to be the acceleration and rapid growth of population in the lowest-income areas of the world; the seeming slowdown of world cereal production; and the growing gap in food production generally between rich and poor areas." Unfortunately for the doomsayers, however, things got a lot better in much of the world after the 1960s, and in very demonstrable ways. "The availability of food increased," says Eberstadt, "and the nutritional status of virtually all of the planet substantially improved, as reflected in further drops in death rates and further increases in life spans."

There are exceptions to this good news, such as in sub-Sahara Africa, but they remain exceptions, and trying to link that region's troubles to "overpopulation" is highly implausible given that Africa is the world's most thinly populated continent. Overall, however, the second half of the last century saw humans living longer and family sizes dropping. It also saw a steady decrease in the inflation-adjusted price of food, a trend that by itself should be the death knell to the Ehrlichean worldview. After all, prices are an objective measure of scarcity, and the price of major cereals have fallen dramatically over the past hundred years, despite the fact that the Earth's population nearly quadrupled between 1900 and 2000.

Economic historian Angus Maddison's *Monitoring the World Economy: 1820–1992* and *The World Economy: A Millennial Perspective* were published by the Organisation for Economic Co-operation and Development in 1995 and 2001, respectively. Students of economic history consider his calculations to be the gold standard, and the trends he documents present a devastating blow to those trying to link population increases to resource reductions.

Between 1900 and 2000, infant mortality rates fell while life expectancy doubled, and the earth's population proceeded to swell from around 1.6 billion to more than 6 billion. Both the rapidity and the magnitude of the growth were unprecedented. It was a full-fledged neo-Malthusian nightmare. Yet over the same period, according to Maddison, global gross domestic product per capita more than quadrupled, and global economic output grew by a factor of eighteen. Remarking on the significance of Maddison's findings, Eberstadt noted, "If the demand for goods and services has multiplied nearly 20-fold during the 20th century, humanity's demand for, and consumption of, natural resources has also rocketed upward. But despite humanity's tremendous new pressures on planetary resources, the relative prices of virtually all primary commodities have fallen over the course of the 20th century, and many of them, quite substantially."

Back in 1980, Julian Simon wagered Ehrlich that Ehrlich and several of his pessimistic colleagues couldn't name any natural resources that would become more expensive over the next decade. Ehrlich and Co. chose copper, chromium, tin, nickel, and tungsten. They lost the bet handily. Every single one of the minerals declined in price. Maddison's research justifies Simon's optimism. Between 1900 and 1998, the price of corn, wheat, and rice fell by 70 percent. Between 1900 and 1999, the price of metals and nonfood agricultural commodities—including aluminum, copper, nickel, zinc, tin, lead, cotton, rubber, palm oil, and wool—also declined. "Suffice then to say," writes Eberstadt, "that the 20th century's population explosion did not forestall the most dramatic and widespread improvement in output, incomes, and living standards that humanity had ever experienced."

The Ultimate Resource

What went on in the twentieth century may be inexplicable in neo-Malthusian theology, but it's little more than the by now predictable workings of the human economy, where people maximize productivity through the augmentation of human resources. Ultimately, it's those human resources rather than natural resources that are the mainspring of wealth, not to mention survival. If you study the laws of thermodynamics you have to be something of a long-term pessimist. The planet has an established mass, more or less. And there's a certain amount of energy that can be derived from that mass. At some level, the earth's resources are surely finite. But while, theoretically, the planet's resources are fixed, no one knows what those fixed amounts are and thus no one can say with any certainty when those resources will be exhausted.

In 1865 the economist William Jevons published *The*

Coal Question, which argued that Britain's industrial growth would be jeopardized by its dwindling coal reserves. But "Jevons failed to anticipate fully the development of substitutes for coal, of new engines, and of other technologies that made more economical use of fuel," writes Nobel economist Gary Becker. Obviously, Jevons's fears were misplaced. Nearly a century and a half has passed, and Britain still hasn't run out of coal.

Or take oil, another natural resource that we're supposedly on the verge of exhausting. In their book, *The Bottomless Well*, Peter Huber and Mark Mills report that U.S. oil fields were scheduled to run dry by the early 1990s, based on a 1979 assessment that only about 30 billion barrels of "proven reserves" remained. "Nevertheless," said the authors, "in the quarter century since 1979, U.S. wells alone yielded another 67 billion barrels." And the United States isn't the only place where predictions have been significantly wide of the mark. According to the American Petroleum Institute, the world's known oil reserves more than doubled between 1969 and 1993.

Humans, incidentally, discovered petroleum more than four thousand years ago, but its potential as a significant energy resource only became apparent in the midnineteenth-century. Until then it was used to make asphalt and fake medicines, among other things. It took human ingenuity to transform a relatively valueless substance into a valuable natural resource. Similarly, we've turned common beach sand into computer chips and optic fiber. Who knew? Who *could* have known? All sorts of things that to-day seem worthless could tomorrow become valuable re-sources, thanks to human ingenuity, which has no obvious limits.

When it comes to the United States, today's greens tend to steer away from fantastic tales of overpopulation-related privation. And rightly so. Our economy has been the world's largest for more than a century and is still bigger than the next three (Japan, Germany, and China) combined. Hence, the ostensibly more reasonable environmental concern put forward vis-à-vis America is that additional residents—im-migrants—will result in more detriment to nature in gen-eral. More global warming. More air and water pollution. More deforestation. More endangered species. More soil ero-sion. More sprawl.

Once again, however, this dour outlook is at war with the facts. To begin with, the United States is nowhere close to being overpopulated. America is a very large country, and the vast majority of it remains quite empty. About 75 percent of the population lives on 3.5 percent of the nation's land. In all, only about 5 percent of America's total land area is even developed. According to a 2006 U.S. Department of Agriculture report, "as of 2002, urban land plus rural resi-dential areas together comprise 154 million acres, or almost 7% of total U.S. land area."

As the economist Thomas Sowell has noted, "In reality, the entire population of the world today could be housed in the state of Texas, in single-story, single-family houses—

four people to a house—and with a typical yard around each home." Don't believe him? Do the math: 7,438,152,268,800 square feet in Texas, divided by the world population of roughly 6,600,000,000, equals 1,126 square feet per person. And in terms of population density, Texas would still be less crowded than the Bronx is today.

Second, and despite what you might have heard about current "record rates of population growth," as the World-watch Institute claimed in 2000, the opposite is happening. The rate of population growth peaked in 1964 at 2.17 percent per year, writes Bjorn Lomborg, a statistician and author of *The Skeptical Environmentalist*. Since then, "the population growth rate has been steadily declining, standing at 1.26 percent in 2000 and expected to drop below 1 percent in 2016. Even the absolute number of people added to the world peaked in 1990 with 87 million. The figure dropped to 76 million added in 2000 and is still decreasing."

We can't predict the future, but we can take (accurate) note of trends. A 2007 UN population report says that as a result of declining fertility and increasing longevity, "the populations of a growing number of countries are aging rapidly. Between 2005 and 2050, half of the increase in the world population will be accounted for by a rise in the population aged 60 or over, whereas the number of children (persons under age 15) will decline slightly."

The seventy-nine countries that are home to 40 percent of the world's people are reporting fertility rates so low that population *decline* may be unavoidable. Yes, China has 1.3 billion people today, but Asia's fertility rate dropped from 2.4 in 1965 to 1.5 in 1995. Over the same period, Latin America's declined from 2.7 to 1.7, and Europe's effectively fell to 0. Worldwide, the typical woman had five children in 1950. In 1995 she had three. The number necessary just to replace the current generation is 2.1.

America is headed in the same general demographic direction, but thanks to our open-border policies, it will take the United States a lot longer to reach the point where immigrant-averse Europe and Asia already have arrived. Between 1950 and 2000, the median age in the United States rose from thirty to thirty-five and is projected to hit forty by 2050. Over the same hundred-year period, however, Europe's median age is expected to jump from twenty-nine to forty-eight, and Japan's, from twenty-two to fifty-three. In forty years, one-third of the population of our major economic competitors—including Germany, Japan, and South Korea—will be over sixty-five, compared to around one-fifth of the U.S. population.

This matters because population trends can directly affect a country's bottom line. The age and growth rate of a nation helps determine its economic prosperity. In 2003, the European Commission's economic and financial affairs division put it this way: "The implications of ageing populations over the coming decades at the global level will be significant in terms of not only a slowdown in the growth rate of output and living standards but also with regard to fiscal and financial market trends . . . falling rates of capital accumulation and a slowdown in productivity growth."

A smaller workforce can mean less overall economic output. Without enough younger workers to replace retirees, health and pension costs can become debilitating. And as domestic markets shrink, so does capital investment. By contrast, younger growing populations expand the market for goods and services. They also spur research and development. Domestic policies that encourage immigration help keep our population not only youthful but vibrant. Immigrants are giving the United States a distinct comparative advantage in human capital, which is no small matter in an increasingly globalized economy.

You Have to Admit It's Getting Better

In 2006, the U.S. population hit the 300 million mark, some thirty-nine years after surpassing 200 million in 1967. Our numbers have swelled by 30 percent since 1975, the biggest growth spurt in our history. The Pew Hispanic Center estimates that about half of that increase is due to immigrants and their U.S.-born children. But for them, our population would be less than 250 million today. So, how's Mother Nature holding up?

For more than a decade the San Francisco–based Pacific Research Institute has issued an annual "Index of Leading Environmental Indicators." The lead author, Steven Hayward, tells me he was inspired by Bill Bennett's *Index of Leading Cultural Indicators*, which tended to focus on bad news—violent crime, illegitimate births, high divorce rates, and the like.

"A lightbulb when off in my head," says Hayward. "I thought to myself, 'What if I did that same treatment for the environment?' It's mostly good news in the U.S., only nobody knows about it. Air pollution is falling, most everything is getting better. Most of the data show improvements, and most of the causes of those improvements are economic growth and technology." As Hayward put it in the introduction to the 2007 edition, "Above all, this index is designed to shine a spotlight on, and deepen our understanding of, environmental *progress*—the side of the environmental story that is seldom told."

The media tends, naturally, to run to green groups for information on the environment. But Greenpeace, the World Wildlife Fund, and the Worldwatch Institute are not objective watchdog organizations, which is how the press often presents them. They have an agenda, and it involves presenting worst-case scenarios for their shock value. A little-publicized Greenpeace faux pas that occurred in 2006 is instructive. The group inadvertently posted an unfinished press release on its Web site, which read in part, "In the twenty years since the Chernobyl tragedy, the world's worst nuclear accident, there have been nearly [FILL IN ALARMIST AND ARMAGEDDONIST FACTOID HERE]."

Green groups are interest groups, too, and as such they tend to present the public with biased information. "My concern," writes the statistician Bjorn Lomborg, "is the asymmetric flow of information that comes from [the media] trusting environmental organizations without the healthy critical angle one would normally put forward had the organizations been, for instance, business conglomerates."

But the bigger problem than bias is that the information coming from these groups is often dead wrong. "The key environmental indicators are increasingly negative," says a 1999 Worldwatch Institute report, even though that statement was plainly untrue at the time and remains so today. According to Hayward's recent indices, the amount of toxic chemicals used in U.S. industry has declined by 60 percent since 1988. Between 1976 and 2001, ambient air pollution levels for lead have dropped by 97 percent; carbon monoxide levels have fallen by 72 percent; and sulfur dioxides by 67 percent.

It gets better. The amount of forest land in the United States actually increased between 1990 and 2002, after being stable since 1920. Between 1982 and 2003, soil erosion rates fell by 43 percent, and the use of "conservation tillage" techniques—to help preserve soil—is more widespread today than ever and continues to expand, so much so that between 1989 and 2004, the percentage of cropland acres *that were not tilled at all* increased from 5.1 to 22.6.

On the global warming front, CO_2 emissions are still rising, but their rate of growth in the United States is declining. Between 1992 and 2000—during the Clinton administration—CO_2 emissions rose 12.8 percent. If current trends hold, between 2000 and 2009—during the Bush administration—they will have grown by half that amount. What's more, the United States has lowered methane emissions substantially in recent years, by 12.8 percent since the 1990 base line year used in the Kyoto Protocol. "This is significant," reports Hayward, "because methane is a more potent greenhouse gas than CO_2—23 times more potent, according to most estimates. The reduction in methane emissions of approximately 4 million tons since 1990 represents the equivalent of a reduction in CO_2 emissions of about 90 million tons."

The greens would have you believe that America's population growth and economic prosperity come at the expense of our ecosystem. That's a curious notion given that the aforementioned positive environmental trends have coincided with tremendous U.S. economic growth. In inflation-adjusted (2000) dollars, the nation's GDP increased by some 227 percent between 1967 and 2006, which, if anything, suggests a positive correlation between economic growth and environmental quality.

As my *Wall Street Journal* colleague Steve Moore has written, "We 300 million Americans are on balance healthier and wealthier and freer than any population ever: We breathe cleaner air, drink cleaner water, earn higher incomes, have more leisure time, and live in less crowded housing. Every natural resource we depend on—water, food, copper and, yes, even oil—is far more abundant today measured by affordability than when our population was 100 million or even 30 million." There's room for improvement, of course, but the notion that immigrants and U.S. population growth are destroying nature is nothing more than a pernicious myth perpetrated by environmentalists and their media enablers.

Moore's optimism is well founded. Each year Dan Esty, director of the Yale Center for Environmental Law and Policy, assembles an "Environmental Performance Index" for the august World Economic Forum. The 2006 edition ranks 133 countries on sixteen indicators tracked in six policy categories—environmental health, air quality, water resources, biodiversity and habitat, productive natural resources, and sustainable energy. Esty writes that, "Wealth and a country's level of economic development emerge as significant determinants of environmental outcomes," and even the most cursory glance at his results bears this out. The world's richest countries tend to receive the highest rankings, while developing nations are concentrated at the bottom. According to Esty, the five most environmentally unfriendly countries on earth are also among the very poorest—Ethiopia, Mali, Mauritania, Chad, and Niger.

In his introduction to an excellent collection of essays

on the environment, *You Have to Admit It's Getting Better*, Terry Anderson says that economic growth "is not the antithesis of environmental quality: rather, the two go hand in hand—if the incentives are right." Anderson, who heads the Property and Environment Research Center, stresses that the right incentives are by-products of the right institutions—property rights, the rule of law, free trade. Those are the prerequisites for creating the wealth that in turn will lead to a cleaner environment, as it has in America and Europe. To the extent that immigrants facilitate U.S. population growth and wealth creation, they are part of the solution, not the problem.

★

CHAPTER TWO

ECONOMICS: HELP WANTED

Republicans in Congress spent the summer of 2006 trying to whip the nation into a frenzy over immigration. The war in Iraq was going south, along with the president's approval rating. More than two out of three voters disapproved of George W. Bush's job performance, and the November mid-term elections were a short way off. The GOP needed an issue to excite its base of supporters—economic and social conservatives who were despondent over ethics scandals and Congress's free-spending ways—and the leadership settled on the illegal immigrant "crisis."

As an issue for Republicans, immigration had potential. It could allow the party to separate itself from an unpopular president, since Bush's position on immigration was closer to the Democrats'. It could also divert attention from the Republican-controlled Congress's own legislative shortcomings and excesses. In late 2005, the House had passed immigration legislation that, among other things, expanded physical barriers along the Mexican border, made unlawful presence in the United States a felony, and increased sanctions on businesses who hire illegal workers. The following spring, the Senate passed its own bill, which was more to Bush's liking because it included not only more enforcement measures but also a guest-worker program for future cross-border labor flows. In addition, the Senate bill allowed illegal aliens in the United States to earn legal status without first returning to their home countries if they met certain requirements—a provision that got the entire Senate bill denounced by opponents as an offer of "amnesty."

Normally, the next step would have been a House–Senate conference to hash out a compromise bill for the president to sign. But Republican leaders gambled that the party had more to gain politically by *not* passing reform legislation and keeping the issue alive for the midterm elections. So instead of conferencing, House Speaker Dennis Hastert announced in June of 2006 that the House would hold a series of nationwide immigration "field hearings" over the next few months to examine the Senate bill. What followed was a summer of political theater worthy of Neil Simon.

Many of the hearings were little more than thinly disguised Republican political rallies, purposely held in congressional districts that were being strongly contested in the upcoming election. Often, they were unabashedly one-sided affairs chock-full of witnesses predisposed to oppose the Senate measure. When GOP Representative Charlie Norwood hosted one such gathering in Gainesville, Georgia, and faced criticism over his unbalanced witness list, he replied in defense and without irony: "What I wanted was witnesses who agree with me, not disagree with me."

Most entertaining of all, however, were the hearings with titles that amounted to loaded questions that answered themselves. A personal favorite was the House Judiciary Subcommittee hearing held in mid-July and titled, "Should We Embrace the Senate's Grant of Amnesty to Millions of Illegal Aliens and Repeat the Mistakes of the Immigration Control and Reform Act of 1986?"

In the event, of course, the gamble didn't pay off politically. That fall, Republicans lost their majority in the House and the Senate. And while the cause can't be laid entirely to the party's hard-line stance on immigration—exit polls said Iraq was the number one issue with voters—it clearly didn't help matters. A Republican Party in control of Congress and the White House had spent the past year making illegal immigration a loud national theme, only to do nothing substantive about the problem. The party thus revealed itself to be either incapable of dealing with the supposed crisis, or incredibly cynical in raising the issue at all.

JOB STEALERS

The political appeal of immigration as a wedge issue, notwithstanding this poor track record, will be discussed later. But the faux hearings of the summer of 2006 help illustrate another recurring claim of immigration opponents, which is that foreign workers displace native workers and lower wages. Immigrants are said to be "stealing" jobs.

GOP Representative Steve King of Iowa put it succinctly after hosting his own hearing that summer. "Nothing good will come from an amnesty bill," he said, referring to the Senate measure. "It will continue to force legal American workers out of their jobs and further deplete the middle class." Mr. King, who as one of Congress's most outspoken restrictionists once compared illegal immigrants to livestock, continued: "I wholly support an immigration policy designed to enhance the economic, social, and cultural well-being of the United States of America. That means employer enforcement and preserving jobs for legal workers." Colorado Congressman Tom Tancredo, another fiery Republican restrictionist, has said that if illegal immigrants were forced out of the country, "thousands of workers and small contractors in the construction industry across Colorado would have their jobs back, the jobs given to illegal workers because they work for lower wages and no benefits."

The argument is also hugely popular with cable newscasters and conservative pundits. CNN's Lou Dobbs says that allowing more foreign-born engineers, medical doctors, and other high-skilled professionals into the country "would force many qualified Americans right out of the job market." Pat Buchanan's beef is with low-skilled migrant labor. In his subtly titled book *State of Emergency: The Third World Invasion and Conquest of America*, Buchanan argues that Latin American newcomers harm the job prospects of working-class natives. Not especially known for his empathy toward the black underclass, Buchanan nevertheless posits that less immigration is a key to black economic advancement. I'm sure the NAACP appreciates his concern.

How the wages and job opportunities of U.S. workers are impacted by foreign migrants is understandably one of the more contentious elements of the immigration debate. The common assumption is that a job filled by an immigrant is one less job for a native. According to this argument, since immigrants increase the supply of labor, not only do they decrease the employment opportunities of native workers but they depress overall wages as well.

Like the overpopulation concern discussed earlier, the full explanation of how immigrants affect the U.S. labor market is more nuanced and somewhat counterintuitive. Hence, opportunistic politicians and media populists have had a field day spooking the masses with misinformation. So in an area of public policy where precise, dispassionate analysis is most needed, we instead have a surfeit of blunt rhetorical instruments.

It's worth noting that during the summer of 2006, while pols like Congressman King were selling economic protectionism to win votes, and cable news yakkers like Bill O'Reilly were doing the same to win ratings, the U.S. economy itself was humming along nicely. Since the Bush tax cuts three years earlier, annual GDP growth had averaged better than 3.6 percent. Consumer spending was also up, which is an indication of consumer confidence in the economy's health. Exports were rising, the budget deficit was falling, inflation was low, and the slowdown predictions of the previous four years hadn't come to fruition.

In the past quarter century there had been only a half-dozen negative GDP quarters, and the last one in 2001 was mild and relatively short-lived. By 2006, the United States was in the fifth year of an economic expansion. No matter how many illegal immigrants are here—and estimates range from 10 million to 12 million and higher—it's hard to convince Americans that Mexican workers are stealing jobs and hurting pay when wages are rising and the unemployment rate is below 5 percent.

Seen through this statistical lens, it's little wonder that immigrant scapegoating failed to resonate with the electorate. Even the most adept populists need some empirical evidence to back up their claims, and the Bush economy of the mid-2000s presented remarkably little data on which to hang anti-immigrant half-truths.

The reality is that America's foreign labor force helps to propel economic growth, not impede it, because the U.S.

job market, properly understood, is not a zero-sum game. The number of jobs in the United States is not static. It's fluid, which is how we want it to be. In 2006, 55 million U.S. workers (or just less than 4.6 million per month) either quit their jobs or were fired. Yet 57 million people were hired over the same period. In a typical year, a third of our workforce is turning over. In about half of those cases the separation is voluntary; in the other half, the worker has been shown the door. But either way, this messy churn, which can disrupt lives and even make obsolete entire industries, has positive macroeconomic consequences in the long run.

That's because flexible labor markets, the kind that minimize the costs to a business of hiring and firing employees, enable workers and employers alike to find the employment situation that suits them best. Flexible labor markets make it easier for an employee who doesn't like a job, is let go, or simply feels underappreciated by his boss to find another position somewhere else. And flexible labor markets make it more likely that an employer will expand his workforce, or take a chance on a job seeker who isn't very skilled or perhaps has a spotty record.

A better fit between employers and employees increases productivity and prosperity and makes markets more responsive to consumer demand. In the end, employers, workers, and consumers are all better off. Immigrants, be they Salvadoran dishwashers, Indian motel operators, or Russian microbiologists, increase the fluidity of U.S. labor markets.

Access to fewer of them would reduce the flexibility that makes America so productive.

A nation's ability to produce goods and services determines its wealth. Productivity, defined as the quantity of goods and services produced from each hour of a worker's time, is why some nations are wealthier than others. It's a major reason why GDP per capita in the United States was $39,676 in 2007, but only $29,300 in France, $6,394 in Ukraine, and $1,237 in Mozambique. Productivity, writes Harvard economist N. Gregory Mankiw, "is the key determinant of living standards" and "the key determinant in growth of living standards." For our purposes, the question is whether immigrant labor ultimately contributes to America's productivity and economic growth, or detracts from it.

Fundamentally, immigration to the United States is a function of a labor shortage for certain kinds of jobs here. Of course, work is not the only reason foreigners migrate to America, but judging from their overrepresentation in the labor force, and the fact that immigrants (excluding refugees) resort to welfare less often than the native-born population, we know that work is the main reason they come.

Rather than appropriating jobs from natives, however, immigrants are more likely to be simply filling them—and often facilitating more employment opportunities in the process. The job-displacement myth, which fuels so much of the national immigration debate, can be rebutted empirically. In 2006, for example, there were around 146 million workers in the United States, and 15 percent, or 21 million, were foreign born. If immigrants are stealing jobs, 21 million U.S. natives, or something approximating that number, should have been out of work. But as economics reporter Roger Lowenstein noted in a July 2006 *New York Times Magazine* article, "the country has nothing close to that many unemployed. (The actual number is only seven million.) So the majority of immigrants can't literally have 'taken' jobs; they must be doing jobs that wouldn't have existed had the immigrants not been here."

The reason that immigrant workers tend not to elbow aside natives for jobs and depress wages has to do with the education and skills that foreigners typically bring to the U.S. labor market. Most immigrants fall into one of two categories: low-skilled laborers or high-skilled professionals. One-third of all immigrants have less than a high school education, and one-quarter hold a bachelor's or advanced degree. Most native workers, by contrast, are concentrated betwixt those two extremes. Hence, immigrant workers tend to act as complements to the native U.S. workforce rather than substitutes. There is some overlap, of course, but this skill distribution is the reason immigrants and natives for the most part aren't competing for the same positions.

A poignant piece of satire that was posted on *The Onion*

Web site makes this point as well as any academic paper—and much more entertainingly. "As millions of new immigrants flood across the border each year," we're told in the ominous intro to a fake, CNN-style report, "the American worker is paying the price." We're then introduced to "Raymond Boyle," a former corporate executive who recently lost his $800,000-a-year job to one "Alberto Fuentes," "who illegally crossed the Arizona–Mexican border in the back of a melon truck two years ago."

The segment goes on to describe how, despite speaking no English and having no formal business education, Fuentes displaced Boyle because Fuentes was "willing to work for significantly less." In no time, the immigrant was outperforming his predecessor, a feat that Fuentes's supervisors attributed to his "ability to put in long hours without taking vacations." Interspersed with shots of the diminutive Fuentes conducting board meetings in a baggy sweatshirt and baseball cap are interviews with Boyle and his family, who've suffered the indignity of having to sell one of their homes. "Unless you've gone through it before," says Boyle, "you can't imagine what it's like to live year-round in your summer home."

The video clip concludes by showing Boyle in his new job busing tables at a TGI Friday's. Of course, that's the kind of job that real-life Alberto Fuenteses typically fill, and their competition is usually a fellow immigrant with similar skills, not a U.S. native. Like the best satire, the segment not only entertains but critiques. And the exaggerations notwithstanding, *The Onion*'s cynical take on immigrants displacing U.S. workers has been validated time and again by the scholarly research.

THE CALIFORNIA EXPERIENCE

A 2007 study published by economist Giovanni Peri analyzed the effects of immigrant labor on California, a state that wasn't chosen arbitrarily. The Golden State, the nation's most populous, is home to nearly a third of all foreign-born U.S. workers. Los Angeles, the nation's second-largest city after New York, is nearly half Hispanic. In the past decade, California's population growth has been almost entirely due to immigration, much of it illegal. The term "Mexifornia" has entered the lexicon. If, as conventional wisdom holds, immigration does in fact have a negative impact on the job security of Americans, California is one of the more likely places that the phenomenon would be manifest.

Yet Peri, a professor of economics at the University of California at Davis, found "no evidence that the inflow of immigrants over the period 1960–2004 worsened the employment opportunities of natives with similar education and experience." With respect to wages, he found that "during 1990–2004, immigration induced a 4 percent real wage increase for the average native worker. This effect ranged from near zero (+0.2 percent) for wages of native high school dropouts and between 3 and 7 percent for native workers with at least a high school diploma." In other words, immigrants tended to expand the economic pie, not displace native workers. These foreign workers lifted all socioeconomic boats; it was just a matter of how much.

At first blush, Peri's findings might seem counterintuitive. It's assumed that because immigrants increase the supply of labor, they necessarily decrease both the wages and the employment opportunities of the native workers. If most immigrant workers were interchangeable with U.S. natives, that might indeed be the case. But the assumption is problematic because immigrants on average aren't stand-ins for natives.

In 2003, the foreign-born share of Ph.D.s working in science and engineering nationwide was 30 percent. Among workers without a high school diploma, the foreign-born share was 23 percent. And among those with only a high school diploma, it was 8 percent. Among native-born U.S. workers, by contrast, some 60 percent had a high school diploma or some college but not a four-year degree.

Peri found that since workers with different levels of education perform different tasks, the majority of native-born workers—high school graduates with some college—experience benefits, more than competition, from the foreign-born workers who are concentrated in high and low educational groups. The result is a more efficient domestic labor market, which leads to more capital investment, higher overall economic growth, and, ultimately, more choices for consumers.

But it also leads to better jobs and higher pay for American workers, explains Peri. "In nontechnical terms," he writes, "the wages of native workers could increase because the increased supply of migrants is likely to put native workers in jobs where they perform supervisory, managerial, training, and . . . coordinating tasks, which makes them more productive." More workers also means more consumers, "so that immigration might simply increase total production and demand without depressing wages."

Peri's findings are hardly anomalous, by the way. Most mainstream economists dismiss this so-called "lump-of-labor" fallacy, which assumes the amount of available work is fixed. An Urban Institute study of immigration's impact on Southern California in the 1970s—a period of high unemployment nationwide, remember—reached a similar conclusion. "To what extent did the influx of immigrants entering Southern California in the 1970s reduce the jobs available to nonimmigrant workers?" wrote Thomas Muller, the study's author. "The answer for the 1970s is little if at all," he concluded. "Despite mass immigration to Southern California, unemployment rates rose less rapidly than in the remainder of the nation." Muller also found that labor-force participation rates among natives seemed to be unaffected, and "the participation rate for both blacks and whites was higher in Southern California [where the bulk of immigrants settled] than elsewhere in the state and the nation."

In 1994 economist Richard Vedder of Ohio University, working with Lowell Gallaway and Stephen Moore, conducted a historical analysis of immigration's impact on the entire U.S. labor force. They found "no statistically reliable correlation between the percentage of the population that was foreign-born and the national unemployment rate over the period 1900–1989, or for just the postwar era (1947–1989)." Moreover, Vedder found that if there is any correlation between immigration and unemployment, it would appear to be negative. Which is to say that higher immigration is associated with lower unemployment.

For example, Vedder found that immigration reached its highest level (relative to population) in the first twenty-five years of the twentieth century, when the average annual unemployment rate was 5.05 percent. Yet over the next sixty-nine years of relatively smaller immigrant flows, the average unemployment rate was 7.38 percent.

Like Peri, Vedder concluded that the reason immigration doesn't cause unemployment is because immigrants help enlarge America's economic pie. "Immigrants expand total output and the demand for labor, offsetting the negative effects that a greater labor supply might have," he writes. "They fill vital niches at the ends of the skill spectrum, doing low-skilled jobs that native Americans rebuff (at prevailing wages) as well as sophisticated high-skill jobs."

Among high-skilled immigrant workers, these dots are perhaps easier to connect. Think of a silicon chip manufacturer in the United States that hires a bright immigrant engineer from China to redesign its products with the goal of making them more cost-efficient and marketable. If the hire is a success, the firm winds up making more chips, which requires more employees. These additional hires—from the managers to the secretaries—are all more likely to be U.S. natives. So are the additional advertisers and marketers who will be sought as the company expands. Why? In part because the skills necessary to do those jobs generally include a familiarity with the native language and culture that a recent immigrant is less likely to possess. As for the American consumer, he's now getting a better product, more choices, and lower prices. Thus has an immigrant hire resulted in more jobs for U.S. natives, not fewer, and increased overall productivity.

"Engineers create jobs," wrote T. J. Rodgers of Cypress Semiconductor in *The Wall Street Journal* a decade ago. "Cypress employs 470 engineers out of 2,771 employees. Each engineer thus creates five additional jobs to make, administer, and sell products he develops." Rodgers noted that a "disproportionate number of our research-and-development engineers—37 percent—are immigrants, typical for Silicon Valley. Had we been prevented from hiring those 172 immigrant engineers, we couldn't have created about 860 other jobs, 70 percent of which are in the U.S."

Of course, high-skill immigrants from Europe, Asia, and Southeast Asia do more than create extra jobs for U.S. employers. They also seem to have a knack for creating entirely new companies that employ thousands of people. Lucky for us. Technology firms, in particular, have made possible the U.S. productivity boom of the past decade. And immigrants have had a hand in starting a disproportionate number of the most successful ones—from Google and eBay to Yahoo! and Sun Microsystems.

A National Foundation for American Policy paper by Stuart Anderson and Michaela Platzer assessed the impact of immigrant entrepreneurs and professionals on U.S. competitiveness. Between 1991 and 2006, they discovered, immigrants started 25 percent of U.S. public companies that were venture-backed. These businesses employed some 220,000 people in the United States and boasted a market capitalization that "exceeds $500 billion, adding significant value to the American economy."

Of course, U.S. colleges and universities educate many of these immigrants who later become entrepreneurs. Which makes it all the more bizarre that restrictionists want to prevent them from coming here in the first place or, barring that, send them back home soon after graduation to work for, or perhaps one day become, a U.S. competitor.

According to the National Science Foundation, students on temporary visas earned just under one-third of all science and engineering doctorates awarded in the United

States in 2003, 55 percent of engineering doctorates, and 43 percent of doctorates in math and computer science. The children of these immigrants, who regularly dominate student math and science competitions, are also an important source of human capital for the United States. In 2004, children of immigrants were 65 percent of the Math Olympiad's top scorers and 46 percent of the U.S. Physics team. That same year, 60 percent of the finalists and seven of the top ten award winners in the Intel Science Talent Search were immigrants or their children. If we had listened to the anti-immigration crowd over the past twenty years, said Stuart Anderson in an interview with *The Wall Street Journal*, "we would have wiped out two-thirds of the top future scientists and mathematicians in the United States because we would have barred their parents from ever entering America."

You'd think that U.S. policy would welcome these talented risk takers—who lately have hailed from places as far-flung as Turkey, Israel, Romania, China, Vietnam, India, and Russia—with open arms. We do, to a certain extent, as evidenced by the fact that the United States remains the predominant destination for foreign students. But our lead has been shrinking in recent years as countries like Australia, Britain, Germany, and France have come to realize the importance of human capital in a global economy and started to compete for it more aggressively.

Indifferent to the trend, Congress chooses to make political hay each year over the number of H-1b visas for skilled professionals that will be issued. The current official cap is sixty-five thousand, an absurdly low number that in recent years has often been reached well before the start of the fiscal year. Opponents of raising the quota or, even better, scrapping it, argue that Silicon Valley is using the visas to hire foreign nationals at lower salaries. But U.S. law requires companies to pay these visa holders prevailing wages and benefits and prohibits hiring them to replace striking Americans. What's more, the government fees and related red tape associated with hiring a foreign professional add thousands of dollars to the process, thus making them more expensive than natives to employ. And since H-1b visas are temporary, additional fees accrue if and when they need to be renewed.

Rather than having Congress pick a number out of thin air (or the latest polls), a better policy route would be to let the market decide how much high-skill foreign labor the economy can accommodate. Indeed, the market already performs this task, when lawmakers get out of the way and let it. Since the H-1b quota was first enacted in 1992, there have been several years when the economy was soft—1992, 2001–2003—and the quota hasn't come close to being met. Lou Dobbs and John Kerry would have you believe that Benedict Arnold CEOs in search of cheap labor are determining the size of our foreign workforce. In fact, it's the law of supply and demand that's making the determination. When U.S. companies can find native workers to fill job openings, they prefer to hire them.

Staying Competitive

If our policy makers want to reduce dependence on foreign professionals without putting U.S. companies at a competitive disadvantage, they would do better to let the free market determine how many foreign workers we need and instead focus their attention on America's K-12 public education system. China is graduating four times as many engineers from college as the United States, and Japan, which has less than half of our population, produces twice as many engineers as we do. Meanwhile, the percentage of incoming undergraduates in the United States planning to major in computer science fell by more than 60 percent between 2000 and 2004 and is 70 percent below its peak in the 1980s.

It's a tragedy that America's public school system is geared more toward appeasing teachers' unions than educating kids. And until that changes, the trends will be difficult to reverse. The upshot of the status quo is that Mumbai and Beijing—often by way of MIT and Stanford—are currently producing a good amount of the talent that Bill Gates needs to keep Microsoft competitive. Immigration policies that limit industry's access to that talent become ever more risky as the marketplace becomes ever more global. If we want American innovators and entrepreneurs to continue enhancing America's wealth and productivity—and if we want the United States to continue as the world's science and technology leader—better to let

Apple and Google and eBay make their own personnel decisions without interference from Tom Tancredo and Lou Dobbs.

With respect to lower-skilled immigrant workers, who are more plentiful and thus more controversial, the economics of the phenomenon don't change. Nor do the end results. True, first-generation Guatemalan whiz kids aren't dominating high school science contests. And their parents are more likely to be manning the assembly line at a meatpacking plant than founding a software company. Still, the low-skilled foreigner, just like his high-skilled counterpart, is contributing to U.S. economic growth. And he, too, is doing so by filling a vital niche in our labor force, only this niche was created by the demographic reality that between 1960 and 2000, the percentage of working-age native born U.S. residents without a high school diploma fell from fifty to twelve.

A construction company, for example, might employ skilled professionals in the form of engineers; intermediate-skilled workers in the form of salesmen, clerks, and accountants; and lower-skilled workers in the form of roofers, plumbers, and crane operators. And just as immigrant computer software engineers expand the labor pool in Silicon Valley, lower-skilled laborers are job multipliers as well. James Holt, a labor economist and former professor at Pennsylvania State University, has found that each farm worker creates three jobs in the surrounding economy—in equipment and sales and processing and packaging. In the forest industry, additional loggers and graders and truck drivers mean additional furniture suppliers and cabinetmakers. Say's Law still applies: Supply creates its own demand.

In 2005 immigrants were 12 percent of the population and 15 percent of the workforce. They were also 21 percent of low-wage workers and 45 percent of workers without a high school education. Around one-third of these immigrant workers were in the country illegally. Yet the U.S. unemployment rate in 2005 averaged just 5.1 percent, a sign that the national labor market for low-wage, low-skilled occupations remains tight, even as fewer and fewer natives are interested in filling the available slots. The strong demand for low-skilled immigrant labor is the result of more and more U.S. natives earning high school and college degrees, which is a good thing. It means more Americans are becoming more productive. But it doesn't follow that the jobs overqualified U.S. natives spurn are now obsolete. Lower-skilled workers, let's remember, tend to manufacture our goods, build our homes, harvest our crops, prepare our food, care for the elderly. They are nannies and janitors and truck drivers and chambermaids. Just because fewer parents are pushing their children toward the building trades doesn't mean the United States has no use for stucco masons.

In fact, the trends point toward the United States needing more of these workers, not fewer, if our economy is to continue expanding. A 2007 Urban Institute study looking at working-age adults without a high school degree found a large drop among natives who fit this profile but an offsetting rise among their immigrant counterparts. Specifically, between 2000 and 2005 the number of native-born adults who lacked a high school diploma fell by about 1 million, while the number of immigrants rose by 900,000. And almost all of that growth in immigrant numbers came by way of illegal aliens.

Foreign-born workers may be only 15 percent of the labor force, but they comprise a disproportionate share of lower-skill occupations like farming (47 percent), construction (27 percent), custodial workers (36 percent), manufacturing (23 percent), and food preparation (24 percent). With the exception of the manufacturing sector, which is expected to continue contracting, these are growth industries that will need more workers in coming years. The Bureau of Labor Statistics expects employment in all occupations to rise by more than 21 million between 2002 and 2012, and higher-than-average demand for jobs that require lower levels of formal education and training. Factor in turnover due to people changing occupations and retiring, and the BLS projection jumps to 56 million new jobs by 2012, or 2.6 job openings for each net new position.

These are the so-called "jobs Americans won't do," a phrase that never fails to get a rise out of restrictionists, who insist that natives would gladly maintain golf courses, chop off chicken heads, and pick cotton in the noonday sun if the pay was better. Their point is well taken but it's still wide of the mark. The issue isn't whether, in the absence of immigrants, we would take it upon ourselves to perform these tasks. If we were to seal off the borders, the market eventually would adjust to the shrinking supply of labor, and wages and prices would adapt. After all, the United States manages to cope when there are shortages of sugar, steel, beef, and other goods.

But as the economic journalist Henry Hazlitt explained, when studying the effects of economic proposals, "we must trace not merely the immediate results but the results in the long run, not merely the primary consequences but the secondary consequences, and not merely the effects on some special group but the effects on everyone." Which is to say that economics is about trade-offs, or making decisions by comparing the costs and benefits of alternative courses of action. So the real question isn't whether living in a closed economy is possible. It's whether the United States is better off moving in a protectionist direction.

Nobel economist Edward Prescott once wrote that protectionism "is seductive, but countries that succumb to its allure will soon have their economic hearts broken." The role of government is not to shield industries and workers from international competition. Latin America and Europe abound with states that have yet to learn this lesson, but restricting the movement of labor and goods can only retard economic growth. Protected goods are more expensive. If Ford and General Motors didn't have competition from Toyota and Honda, cars would be more expensive and fewer people could afford them.

Closing off the U.S. economy to foreign labor likewise would have negative consequences, primarily because the country would have less human capital overall. What's more, we'd be a poorer society because we'd be using the human capital we did have less efficiently. Low-skilled immigrants fill millions of jobs in agriculture, construction, hotels, health care, light manufacturing, and retail. These are big and important sectors of the U.S. economy, and businesses depend on immigrant labor to stay competitive. Again, the issue isn't so much the viability of removing foreign labor from the U.S. economy. We'd manage. The issue is whether America would be better off with an immigration policy that incentivizes natives to take jobs below their skill level.

At some higher wage, there would be more Americans harvesting tomatoes, hanging drywall, and applying for chambermaid positions at Hilton. Prices matter. And the willingness of Americans to do a job depends on how much the position pays. But at the same time, businesses can't raise salaries without regard for what consumers are willing to pay for goods and services, which is why we can't raise the minimum wage to twenty-five dollars an hour and—*poof!*—eliminate poverty. Agribusiness would certainly attract more Americans if field hands made fifty thousand dollars a year, but not without also affecting the price of food. Not only would we have to pay more for groceries, but higher food prices would rebound to the restaurant industry, for example, since fewer people would eat out.

Restrictionists also assume that all of these jobs would exist in the absence of the immigrants who now fill them, but that's not how labor markets work. Seal the border, and you don't get the same number of jobs at higher salaries. What you get instead are fewer jobs overall. One of the bigger disruptions would be in light manufacturing, where businesses would likely opt to close or move overseas if the immigrant labor supply were cut off. The only reason our textile industry still exists is because textile mills in places like North Carolina and Georgia have had access to immigrant labor. The same holds true for meatpacking plants in the Midwest. And there are other examples. "The restaurant industry is the country's largest private sector employer with 12.5 million people," says John Gay of the National Restaurant Association. "We project we're going to add 15 percent to that number of job slots in the next ten years. But the 16–24 age group that makes up half of our industry's workforce isn't growing at all over ten years. If we don't find a way for our industry to get more workers—and we're not the only ones in this boat—we're going to be in a world of hurt."

Pia Orrenius, a senior economist at the Federal Reserve Bank of Dallas who has analyzed the effects of Latin American immigration, agrees. "Basically, a lot of these jobs would not exist at higher wages, and that would affect our economic well-being," says Orrenius. "You wouldn't have people manicuring nails if it costs $200 to have it done. And if you want the college-educated sitting down and doing nails, that's what it would take to make it worth their time." Of course we don't want that, says Orrenius. "Because if you have high-skilled natives doing low-productivity jobs, it's a fundamental misallocation of labor and a big inefficiency. And it makes people—natives—worse off."

Yes, there are Americans with low skills to fill these jobs. The problem is that the number of such Americans is steadily shrinking, which is a good thing. Orrenius's point is that we don't want people doing jobs that they're overqualified for. That leads to inefficiencies in the labor market. The fear is that if low-skill foreigners aren't available to fill certain jobs and perform certain services, those jobs and services will either go away or be filled by overqualified individuals who will demand high salaries to fill them. (In much of Europe, for example, dry-cleaning is a luxury, and inflexible labor markets are the reason.)

The labor shortage in agriculture is such that some 20 percent of crops were left at the farm gate in 2006. The problem was expected to worsen in 2007, since the number of government raids had increased and most farm workers are illegal aliens. Restrictionist lawmakers, talk radio, and the editors of *National Review* keep assuring us that wages for field hands eventually will rise to a level where over-qualified natives will be induced to pick lettuce in Yuma and weed fields in the lower Rio Grande Valley. But that's not what's happening.

American growers who live in the real world and need

to stay competitive have other options, one of which is to offshore, or move production outside of the United States. Tim Chelling of the Western Growers Association, whose three thousand members in California and Arizona generate half of the nation's fresh produce, tells me that in recent years a number of large-scale growers have relocated some of their operations south of the border, in places like Mexicali Valley, Caborca, and Baja. "There's a quiet exodus going on already, tens of thousands of acres and millions of dollars in economic activity," says Chelling. "Growers are saying, 'If you won't give me a legal labor force here, then I'll go where the labor force is legal.'"

This isn't about immigrants displacing Americans in the labor force. It's about foreign workers coming here to fill jobs that the natives don't want because they've got better opportunities. Regarding agriculture, foreigners are going to do the work in any case. It's just a question of whether the jobs and attendant economic activity are generated here or somewhere else. The reality is that U.S. companies will either grow food domestically that is harvested by foreign workers, or import food harvested by foreign workers.

AUTOMATION NATION?

Some have argued that the availability of cheaper immigrant labor harms productivity by delaying automation in certain industries. "By not enforcing the immigration laws," says agriculture economist Philip Martin, "the government is sending a signal to farmers that by hiring unauthorized workers they do not have to make a transition to a more mechanized, higher productive agriculture." In a 2001 study, Martin said that the termination of the Bracero Program for Mexican guest-workers in 1964 led to the automation of tomato picking. "In the tomato case," he concluded, "the end of the Bracero Program led to the mechanization of the tomato harvest, expanding production, and a reduction in the price of processed tomato products, which helped to fuel the fast-food boom."

Martin and others are right to note that immigration has slowed mechanization in certain sectors of the economy. But their argument presupposes that every activity that can be automated should be, as if the most efficient course is to keep all manual workers outside of developed countries. Does the availability of cashiers retard technological innovations in the retail sector that could produce universal self-service checkout? Not necessarily. To use Martin's example, time and money spent trying to come up with machines to duplicate a low-skill human activity could have been directed at other improvements, such as developing healthier varieties of tomatoes (rather than varieties that can be recognized by machines). Furthermore, the tomatoes are still being picked by machines at a higher cost than if you allowed a sizeable number of guest-workers to do the job—and with no clear economic gain for Americans. For-

eign workers who are less productive in their home countries could be more productive here. And unlike the
machines, immigrants not only pick produce but also consume products and services, thus helping the U.S. economy
expand.

Another politically popular argument is that sealing the
southern border and giving Mexican immigrants the boot
would be a boon to low-skilled Americans. You will not
search the academic literature in vain for studies showing
that immigrants dampen the labor market outcomes of the
lowest-skilled natives. But neither will you find an abun-
dance of research that comes to that conclusion. It's true
that these immigrants compete most directly with U.S. natives who lack a high school degree. But it's also true that
the percentage of Americans so educated has been sharply
declining in absolute terms for decades. Keep in mind, too,
that even absent competition from foreign workers, this
group would still have to compete for jobs in a marketplace
that increasingly places a premium on skills.

The pinup economist for immigration hawks is Harvard's
George Borjas, whose research has found that high immigration is associated with slower wage growth among lower-
skilled native workers. Borjas doesn't argue that foreign
workers "steal" jobs and even concedes that immigration's
overall impact on the U.S. economy is positive—that on average, American wages are higher because of immigrants—
though both points usually go unmentioned by immigration
critics who trot out his studies in support of their position.

In fact, Borjas has found that immigration increases GDP by 0.2 percent, or some $22 billion per year. That amount may seem trifling in a multitrillion-dollar U.S. economy, but it's significant when compounded over time. And as the economist Benjamin Powell has noted, the same conservative restrictionists who downplay that gain would cheer the abolition of hundreds of government regulations that might have significantly smaller economic effects.

But never mind. In a 2003 paper, Borjas concluded that in the years 1980–2000, real wages fell by around 9 percent for unskilled U.S. natives, and this finding has been treated as gospel in anti-immigration circles ever since. To produce that number, however, Borjas had to rig his model. In particular, he assumed that physical capital is fixed—that the number and size of companies in the United States is constant—and that immigrants are perfect substitutes for natives. When you increase labor in an economy where investment doesn't adjust, wages fall because workers are less productive. This was the methodology he employed to produce the 9 percent result that so delights immigrant foes.

The only problem with trying to determine the impact of immigration over two decades by assuming capital doesn't change over time is that it bears no resemblance whatsoever to how the U.S. economy actually functions. It's like trying to ease traffic congestion by assuming flying carpets are an option. The reality is that investors are constantly responding to the inflow of immigrant labor.

These additional workers increase the return on capital, spurring more investment. Companies respond by producing more labor-intensive goods. And all of this activity only serves to lighten any adverse impacts on low-skill native workers.

Indeed, in the very same 2003 study, Borjas presents alternate findings that control for increased investment, and that 9 percent wage loss for high school dropouts suddenly falls to 5 percent. Two years later, the National Bureau of Economic Research published a paper co-authored by Borjas and Lawrence Katz on the effects of Mexican immigrants. By realistically allowing capital to adjust, they found even less of a negative effect on wages (4 percent).

Other research has shown little, if any, adverse impact on low-skilled Americans. Back in 1990, David Card of the University of California at Berkeley produced a widely read paper on how the influx of Cuban refugees during the 1980 Mariel Boatlift affected Miami's labor market. Card found that although Mariel immigrants increased Miami's workforce overall by 7 percent, and the percentage increase in labor supply to unskilled occupations was even greater, "the Mariel influx appears to have had virtually no effect on the wages or unemployment rates of less-skilled workers." A 1995 study by the economists Rachel Friedberg and Jennifer Hunt states flatly, "The popular belief that immigrants have a large adverse impact on the wages and employment opportunities of the native-born population of the receiving country is not supported by the empirical evidence." The authors add that "even those natives who are the closest substitutes with immigrant labor do not suffer significantly as a result of increased immigration. There is no evidence of economically significant reductions in native employment."

Pia Orrenius and Madeline Zavodny, a labor economist at Agnes Scott College, found that immigration to the United States in the mid- to late 1990s depressed the wages of manual laborers by about 1 percent. And research by economist Gianmarco Ottaviano and Giovanni Peri found that when you consider (as discussed earlier) that immigrants and natives aren't necessarily interchangeable but often complement one another in the labor force, the negative impact on low-skill natives is even further diminished.

Helping Blacks

Of course, no "significant" negative impact is not the same as no negative impact at all. And some protectionists argue that, however small the repercussions, immigration should be curtailed for the benefit of those Americans who compete most directly with low-skilled foreign workers for entry-level jobs. Black Americans, who are disproportionately concentrated in low-skilled jobs, are considered especially vulnerable. The black unemployment rate is typically double that of whites and significantly higher among black males. Can this situation be laid to immigrants?

Two years ago, when a prominent black minister in Chicago told *The New York Times* that "immigration will destroy the economic base of the African-American community," he joined a long queue of restrictionist black leaders and intelligentsia. As Congress debated the Chinese Exclusion Act of 1882, a number of black newspapers called for its passage, including the *Colored American* in Washington, D.C., which wrote, "There is no room for these disease-breeding, miserly, clannish, and heathen Chinese." Later, W. E. B. Du Bois and Booker T. Washington would complain that immigrant labor was pushing blacks out of manufacturing jobs. The black separatist Marcus Garvey—an immigrant from Jamaica, by the way—and sworn enemy of more mainstream civil rights leaders like Du Bois and A. Philip Randolph, nevertheless found common ground with them when it came to railing against the Eastern Europeans who were pouring into Northern cities in the first part of the twentieth century.

Others at the time, like the influential Immigration Restriction League, an early-twentieth-century nativist group comprised of white Northerners, disingenuously cited "the welfare of the negro" as a chief reason to oppose immigration. Today, vigilante groups like the Minuteman Project make similar claims, notwithstanding their links to white nationalists and the prominent presence of Confederate flags at their rallies.

The persistence of this uneasy relationship between immigrants and some in the black community was illustrated in a 2006 episode involving Andrew Young, the one-time Martin Luther King Jr. confidante and civil rights icon. Young had been retained by Wal-Mart to help the company fend off attacks from labor unions and politicians. And when a reporter from a black newspaper asked him about the retail giant displacing mom-and-pop stores in black neighborhoods, Young responded by trying to shift the target of animus from Wal-Mart to Jewish, Korean, and Arab immigrant merchants "overcharging us, selling us stale bread and bad meat and wilted vegetables," among other things. "I think they've ripped off our communities enough," said Young. "Very few black people own these stores."

Young immediately apologized and resigned his post. And although his comments understandably caused a short-lived media tempest, many black Americans wondered what all the fuss was about. Reacting to the brouhaha, a commentator on National Public Radio noted matter-of-factly, "Truth is, in my world, Los Angeles, most of the mom-and-pop stores in the predominantly black sections are owned by Koreans and Jews. And they do overcharge and they tend to be rude and hostile to their black customers. And the blacks employed in these shops are most often not allowed to handle the cash register. The overall result of this environment is a long history of bad attitudes, scuffles, and even one death. What pains me is that Andrew Young stated this truth, then apologized."

Such thinking was also behind the Detroit city council's decision in 2004 to approve a racially exclusive business district for black entrepreneurs. The premise of the proposal, which was legally suspect and ultimately rejected, was that immigrants from Latin America and the Middle East were taking jobs and resources that otherwise would be going to black natives.

In last year's debate Congressional Black Caucus members at one point visibly broke with Latino colleagues, who are normally strong allies. During a House Judiciary hearing, black members berated representatives from the restaurant industry, agriculture, and Google with questions like: "My son goes to Morehouse College. Have you gone there recruiting?" and "Have you tried to employ urban black workers for agriculture jobs?" and "What percentage of your employees are black Americans?"

To finger immigrants for the high rate of black unemployment and the dearth of black business start-ups, however, is to ignore a host of much more likely cultural, economic, and political culprits. The reality is that inner-city grocers charge more for food because they have relatively higher operating costs and less competition than big supermarket chains with economies of scale. And, more fundamentally, high jobless rates among black natives—and black males especially—has much more to do with their unemployability than the lack of available jobs.

Two economists with the Urban Institute, Harry Holzer and the late Paul Offner, found that employment rates for black men between sixteen and twenty-four actually dropped in the 1990s, a decade of strong economic growth and job creation. Among the primary reasons cited for low labor participation rates in this subgroup were declining real wages, a significant skills gap between black and white workers, high black incarceration rates, and the disappearance of manufacturing and other blue-collar jobs in recent decades. Holzer and Offner also reported that "employers perceive a stronger work ethic among immigrants of all racial groups, and a greater willingness to accept and retain low-skill jobs."

A front-page *Wall Street Journal* story in 2006 provided a useful real-world illustration of the latter point. After federal immigration officials raided the Crider chicken-processing plant in Georgia, the company lost 75 percent of its nine hundred workers, who were mostly Latino immigrants. Local black residents quickly filled the openings, and for the first time since the late 1990s black workers dominated Crider's processing line. Inside of six months, however, the company's racial and ethnic makeup reverted to the migrant-dominant preraid norm. "The plant has struggled with high turnover among black workers, lower productivity, and pay disputes between the new employees and labor contractors," according to the *Journal*. "The allure of compliant Latino workers willing to accept grueling conditions despite rock-bottom pay has proved a difficult habit for Crider to shake, particularly because the local, native-born workers who replaced them are more likely to complain about working conditions."

Restrictionists point to places like Crider and see an argument for sealing the border. But it's hardly prudent to fashion America's immigration policy around protecting a small and dwindling bloc of workers whose circumstances lend themselves to so many alternative explanations. And given that, on balance, those foreign laborers are expanding the economic pie by creating better-paying jobs for an ever-growing number of natives with higher skills, the greater good is surely served by keeping the welcome mat in place.

The U.S. economy today rewards education and job skills. The stagnation of wages at the lower rung serves as a market signal that encourages people to stay in school and upgrade their skills. It tells people that if you want to prosper in your adult life, you should get an education. And that—rather than keeping out ambitious if undereducated immigrants—will be the key to the country's economic success going forward.

If lawmakers want to encourage more black entrepreneurship in the ghetto and improve the job prospects of working-class blacks, deregulating the marketplace would be far more effective than removing low-skill immigrants from the labor mix. Up until 1950 or so, and in an era of open and rampant racial discrimination, the jobless rate for young black men was much lower than today and not very different from whites in the same age group. Today's unemployment gap has less to do with immigrants (or racism) than with the implementation of various labor regulations, such as the federal minimum wage laws put in place in the 1930s.

Before then, the wages of inexperienced and unskilled workers were determined by supply and demand. Because there was no federal minimum wage—and because unions typically did not organize inexperienced and unskilled workers—such individuals were able to find employment much like everyone else.

But that would change in the 1930s. The Davis-Bacon Act of 1931 established the requirement for paying prevailing (read: union) wages on public works projects. It was passed in part to stop black laborers from displacing whites by working for less money. Politicians at the time were explicit about their aim to exclude blacks from federal contracts. During the floor debate, Missouri Representative John Cochran said he had "received numerous complaints in recent months about Southern contractors employing low-paid colored mechanics getting work and bringing the employees from the South." And Alabama Representative Clayton Allgood told the story of a "contractor from Alabama who went to New York with bootleg labor. This is a fact. That contractor has cheap colored labor that he transports, and he puts them in cabins, and it is labor of that sort that is in competition with white labor throughout the country."

Today, just 18 percent of construction workers are unionized, yet Democratic politicians, genuflecting to the AFL-CIO, have kept Davis-Bacon in place to protect them. Because most blacks in construction aren't unionized, however, the law has the effect of freezing them out of jobs. It also has the effect of significantly increasing the costs of government projects, since there are fewer contractors to bid on them than there would be absent Davis-Bacon.

In 1938, Congress passed the Fair Labor Standards Act, which established a national minimum wage. Milton Friedman said he regarded "the minimum wage as one of the most, if not the most, anti-black laws on the statute books." In *Capitalism and Freedom*, he wrote that "minimum wages laws are about as clear a case as one can find of a measure the effects of which are precisely the opposite of those intended by the men of good will who support it." Proponents maintain that outlawing wage rates below a certain government-mandated level is an effective way of reducing poverty. In fact, such laws are much more effective at reducing employment. Younger and less-skilled workers, who tend to be minorities, are priced out of the labor market altogether. And if you can't get an entry-level job, you can't gain the skills and experience needed to move up the economic ladder.

The irony is that these laws so detrimental to blacks

survive today with the strong support of black lawmakers. When it comes to campaign contributions, Big Labor gives generously to the Congressional Black Caucus, as well as black Democratic politicians at the state and local level. In return, the black political left, with very few exceptions, endorses the union agenda, even when it undermines the welfare of their black constituents.

The same holds true in the area of education. The U.S. economy today, more so than at any time in the past, places a premium on skills. Yet black seventeen-year-olds read on the level of white thirteen-year-olds and persistently lag far behind whites on aptitude tests. Considering that black children also watch more TV, read fewer books, and are overrepresented in the worst public schools in the country, those findings shouldn't come as a surprise. What's truly jarring is that so many black lawmakers, from Congressmen on down, support policies that keep black children stuck in those failing schools. In deference to the National Education Association teachers' union, which is anathema to school choice, the black political class works diligently to block black access to vouchers and charter schools and other reforms that could facilitate a decent education. Before blaming the diminished job prospects of Jamal on Jorge, blacks would do better to address the anti-intellectualism that permeates the culture of the black underclass. And legislators might first consider revisiting the racially tinged protectionist laws and public policies already on the books.

FRENCH LESSONS

Living in a free-market society inevitably involves living with more economic risk. The effects of business cycles can be minimized but not eliminated. The disequilibrium that characterizes our economy is also what makes possible the innovation and productivity that facilitate our prosperity. The welfare states of continental Europe offer another model for managing an economy. Italy, Germany, and France feature highly protected labor markets, where the interest of the worker is placed above that of the consumer. Europe's universal health care, thirty-five-hour work weeks, and six-week vacation mandates make America's political left go gaga. But protectionism has a considerable downside; for decades, the Continent has had consistently higher unemployment and lower productivity than what's found in the United States.

Take France, which sports the slowest-growing large economy in the European Union, the fastest-rising public debt in Western Europe, and entrenched high unemployment. In the early 1980s, French GDP per person was the seventh-highest in the world. By 2007 it had fallen to seventeenth place. "The most urgent cure for all these ills is to get the economy growing faster," advises *The Economist* magazine. "That requires radical liberalisation of labour and product markets, more competition and less protection, lower taxes and cuts in public spending, plus a shake-up of the coddled public services."

If you know you can't fire unproductive employees, you become overly cautious in taking on new workers. There's less risk-taking in general. That additional worker is less likely to be hired and the company expands at a slower pace, or not at all. The more regulated the marketplace, the higher the entry costs. Entrepreneurs and investment capital flee to friendlier places. Which means fewer new businesses, less competition for existing firms, higher costs for consumers, and slower overall economic growth. In France, the system is stacked against anyone who doesn't already have a job. The beauty of flexible labor markets is that they fuel growth and job creation, so displaced workers can more easily rejoin the labor pool.

Restrictionists fret that the tanned influx from Latin America has the United States slouching toward Guatemala. But the bigger concern is that without those immigrants, and the job mobility they catalyze, the United States risks slouching toward France.

---★---

CHAPTER THREE

WELFARE:
THE MEASURE OF A MANUEL

In the spring of 2007 the Council on Foreign Relations, long a font of center-left received wisdom, published a paper by Gordon Hanson titled "The Economic Logic of Illegal Immigration." Hanson is an economist at the University of California at San Diego, and the paper's somewhat cheeky thesis is that, from a purely economic standpoint, undocumented immigrants do a much better job of responding to the demands of the U.S. labor market than their lawful counterparts. It is frequently said that legal immigrants are a net benefit for the economy and that illegal immigrants are a net drain. But Hanson turns that notion on its head.

Obviously, there are very good reasons to reduce the

illegal alien population in the United States, and chief among them is national security. As of this writing, no terrorist attacks in the United States can be tied to anyone who illicitly forded the Rio Grande, but it's only prudent to minimize that possibility. Human smuggling, document fraud, and corpses in the Arizona desert are other major problems associated with illegal border crossings, and a later chapter will address how U.S. immigration policy might best address those kinds of concerns.

Hanson's paper, however, is narrowly focused on whether our economic welfare is helped or harmed by porous borders. He looks at the fiscal costs and benefits of illegal immigrants and how they compare with those newcomers who use the front door. "This analysis concludes that there is little evidence that legal immigration is economically preferable to illegal immigration," writes Hanson. "In fact, illegal immigration responds to market forces in ways that legal immigration does not."

How's that? To begin with, illegal immigrants are more sensitive to the U.S. business cycle. They tend to come when the economy is expanding, and they can more easily migrate to those areas of the country where job growth is fastest because they're not bound to a single employer. Legal immigrants necessarily respond more slowly to economic conditions. The number of green cards available each year is fixed, and the backlog is several years long. The bureaucratic calendar, rather than market demand, determines the flow of foreign workers.

Even temporary legal immigrants aren't as flexible and mobile as illegals, since temporary visa holders can't change jobs without permission from their employer. And while the quotas on temporary legal immigrants are ostensibly linked to economic need, adjustments in the number of available visas have lagged job growth by as much as thirty-six months, and the determining factor has usually been Congress's political mood, not labor market signals.

Hanson lists the manifold benefits that accrue in the U.S. economy from these foreign workers—especially the illegal ones. By augmenting the supply of available resources, "immigration raises the productivity of resources that are complementary to labor," he writes. "More workers allow U.S. capital, land, and natural resources to be exploited more efficiently. Increasing the supply of labor to perishable fruits and vegetables, for instance, means that each acre of land under cultivation generates more output. Similarly, an expansion in the number of manufacturing workers allows the existing industrial base to produce more goods."

The restrictionists reply that natives would gladly perform these tasks if low-skill immigrants weren't available. But that misses the point, which is that Americans are increasingly overqualified for the sorts of jobs Latino immigrants are filling. Sure, a U.S. native with a high school diploma or some college could work as a field hand, but that's probably not the best use of his skills. And if he's picking strawberries on a California farm, or busing tables at an Applebee's in Texas, or working the production line of an Iowa chicken-processing plant, it means he's not doing a job he's better suited for. And since his labor is more expensive, it also means he's raising the costs of production in those industries, which leads to higher prices for consumers and a less productive workforce overall. As was discussed earlier, low-skill immigrants ultimately increase the incomes of natives by allowing our free-market economy to allocate human capital and other domestic resources more efficiently.

Hanson's paper also analyzes the economic *costs* associated with illegal immigration. There's downward pressure on the wages of native workers who compete directly for jobs with immigrants (though, again, there's a dwindling number of natives vying for such jobs). But the author's real concern is the direct fiscal costs of these newcomers to ordinary Americans. Do illegal aliens pay less in taxes than they received in public benefits? Are they snouts at the trough, burdening taxpayers through heavy use of welfare services?

Even for economists, who relish performing complicated calculations, determining the fiscal consequences of immigration is an exceptionally difficult challenge. Estimates vary widely based on who's immigrating, their age at arrival, the number of offspring, the skill sets, the education level, the public benefits at stake, and other factors. Like most researchers who've looked at the issue of immigrant "costs," Hanson concludes that, on balance, it's a wash. Some immigrants are net contributors to the public fisc; others are net beneficiaries. But in the end, fiscally speaking, immigrants don't make a big impact on the nation's purse.

Still, it's worth examining this argument further. What does it mean to cite welfare costs as a reason to restrict immigration? Those who do are suggesting that a person's worth to society is nothing more than the sum of his tax payments. By that standard, however, most natives are "worthless," since some 60 percent collect more in government services than they pay in taxes. This doesn't mean that six out of ten Americans are conscientious moochers; the phenomenon can be laid to our highly progressive tax system, where the top 1 percent of earners is responsible for 37 percent of federal income tax payments. Even so, it would be foolhardy to argue that 60 percent of Americans are fiscally expendable and that the United States would be better off without them because they don't "pay their way."

Such reductionism ignores the propensity of foreign workers to save and start new businesses at higher rates than natives, which contributes to the economic welfare of the nation. Low-skill immigrants also have a higher labor-force participation rate than natives and a lower rate of unemployment. Lower-income workers, whether foreign-born or American, enable large sectors of the economy—farming, construction, manufacturing, health care—to function and grow. And in the process they create job opportunities for the rest of us.

Snouts at the Trough?

We sometimes refer in the United States to the presence of the "welfare state," but that term needs context. Europe, for example, spends twice as much on social programs as we do, and assistance aimed at the poor and the unemployed is especially generous. So, too, in the main, are European public pensions—wealth-redistribution mechanisms that effectively take from the affluent young and give to the disadvantaged old. In the end, total government spending on the Continent approaches a world-leading 50 percent of GDP, versus about 30 percent in the United States. And unlike in the United States, Europe's welfare system helps keep immigrants and their children out of the labor force, which weakens their incentive to assimilate. The United States and Europe are both "welfare states" in the same way that Tiger Woods and the teaching pro at a country club are both good golfers. It's technically true, but the orders of magnitude that separate them deserve more precise explanations.

This U.S.–Europe welfare disparity, to a large extent, reflects the different attitudes and preferences that prevail on opposite sides of the Atlantic. Polls show that Europeans tend to view the poor as hard-luck cases who aren't personally responsible for their situation, while Americans tend to view welfare recipients as, well, shiftless cheats. Income inequality bothers Europeans much more than Americans, which annoys U.S. liberals to no end. But it makes sense when you consider that large majorities in the United States—71 percent, according to one survey—see poverty as a condition that can be overcome by dint of hard work, while just 40 percent of Europeans share that viewpoint.

Belief in social mobility has informed U.S. welfare and immigration policy from colonial times. In 1645 the Massachusetts Bay colony was already barring paupers. And more than two centuries later, in 1882, when Congress finally got around to passing the country's first major piece of immigration legislation, it specifically prohibited entry to "any person unable to take care of himself or herself without becoming a public charge."

Welfare has become a much-abused term in the immigration debate. The common notion of welfare is a set of cash-transfer programs for people who can't work. That's generally what leading social scientists like Charles Murray and William Julius Wilson were writing about during the welfare debates of the 1980s and 1990s. When it suits their purposes, however, immigrant detractors expand welfare's meaning to include everything from the use of roads and public schools, to fire and police protection, health-care benefits, and defense spending.

Historically, neither capitalists nor conservatives have been opposed to welfare per se, though they generally favor its private and informal manifestations—churches, benevolent associations, extended families—over the government variety. Still, even Republicans have accepted welfare programs as a sort of temporary insurance policy—a safety net—for victims of hardship or misfortune. The consensus, on the left and right, is that it's acceptable for the government to provide for the aged and disabled, or to allow someone to receive an unemployment check while searching for a new job.

Conservative revisionists may try to blame it all on the political left, but the American version of the welfare state that emerged between the 1930s and 1970s was a result of bipartisan efforts. A Democratic president, Franklin Delano Roosevelt, is the face of the New Deal. But many of the initiatives of that period—including Social Security, Aid to Families with Dependent Children, and Unemployment Insurance—actually originated with Republican state governors and FDR's GOP predecessor, Herbert Hoover. It was Dwight Eisenhower, another Republican, who launched the Cabinet-level Department of Health, Education, and Welfare in 1953. And although a Democratic president, Lyndon Johnson, gave us the Great Society, its programs expanded exponentially during the Republican administrations of Richard Nixon and Gerald Ford.

Welfare becomes a problem when people become habituated to it, when dependency isn't kept to a minimum and benefits become more attractive than a paycheck. The historical tendency to keep immigrants out of welfare programs began to fade during the War on Poverty in the 1960s. Means-tested programs were added and enhanced but legislation was usually silent on whether citizenship was required to participate. Some states moved to bar noncitizens from public assistance, but a 1971 Supreme Court decision, *Graham v. Richardson*, reversed those efforts, holding that only the federal government could regulate immigrants' use of welfare. Between 1970 and 1980, more than forty welfare programs grew at a rate that was three times as fast as wages and more than twice as fast as the GDP.

Illegal aliens, who are one-third of all immigrants, do not have access to federal welfare benefits. And many illegals are reluctant to take advantage of the emergency health care available to them out of fear of apprehension by the authorities. Immigrant bashers who like to drag the undocumented population into the cost debate often leave out these inconvenient facts, either out of ignorance or an acute sense that it undermines their argument. The truth is this: Because the illegals who collect a paycheck also pay payroll and Social Security taxes but are denied the attendant benefits, Uncle Sam tends to come out ahead.

Among legal immigrants, however, welfare use began rising steadily after the 1960s. The major federal benefits programs are Supplemental Security Income (SSI), the Food Stamp Program (FSP), Medicaid, and Temporary Assistance for Needy Families (TANF). And noncitizen use of these programs continued to grow in recent decades, both in absolute numbers and as a percentage of the total. In 1984, noncitizens were 4.5 percent of SSI caseloads. By 1995 they were more than 12 percent. Similarly, immigrant enrollment in TANF grew from 7 percent to 12.3 percent between 1989 and 1996. And foreign nationals were 4.4 percent of food stamp recipients in 1989 versus 7.1 percent in 1996.

Had welfare become a magnet for lazy foreigners to come here and live on the dole? High immigrant work rates, among other indicators, strongly argued otherwise. The more likely explanation is that more immigrants were receiving public assistance because welfare activists and liberal policy makers were actively recruiting them. States went so far as to engage in official outreach efforts. Illinois state employees were tasked with venturing into immigrant neighborhoods to enroll people in health benefit programs. It seems utterly cruel, from a public policy standpoint, for the United States to invite foreigners to participate in welfare and then hold it against them when they take us up on the offer. If welfare use among immigrants is deemed too high, then the better course of action is to limit the benefits, not the immigrants who are otherwise enhancing the nation's economic vigor.

And that's exactly what federal lawmakers eventually did. In 1996 the Republican Congress passed and President Clinton signed (after twice vetoing it) comprehensive welfare reform legislation that was aimed in part at weaning immigrants off the public teat. The Personal Responsibility and Work Opportunity Act barred noncitizens from receiving most means-tested federal aid for at least five years following entry. As intended, immigrant use of these programs subsequently plummeted. Between 1995 and 2001, noncitizen enrollment in TANF, food stamps, SSI, and Medicaid dropped by 55 percent, 52 percent, 45 percent, and 22 percent, respectively. Medicaid enrollment, by contrast, has since increased—as of 2004, it was up by more than 30 percent since 1994—mainly because states have elected to exercise their option to continue coverage and even expand immigrant eligibility.

Some immigration detractors, such as Robert Rector of The Heritage Foundation, claim that even though illegal immigrants themselves don't qualify for federal welfare benefits, their U.S.-born children, who are citizens, do. Therefore, according to Rector, illegal immigration is indirectly driving welfare caseloads. Sounds plausible, but is it true?

Between 1995 and 2004, America's illegal immigration population is estimated to have doubled to around 12 million. Yet Peter Wehner and Yuval Levin report in the December 2007 issue of *Commentary* magazine that welfare caseloads over that period are not just down but down dramatically. "Since the high-water mark in 1994, the national welfare caseload has declined by 60 percent. Virtually every state in the union has reduced its caseload by at least a third, and some have achieved reductions of over 90 percent."

Apparently, immigrants don't drive up welfare caseloads any more than they drive down U.S. employment. The authors go on to note that, "Not only have the numbers of people on welfare plunged, but, in the wake of the 1996 welfare-reform bill, overall poverty, child poverty, black child poverty, and child hunger have all decreased, while employment figures for single mothers have risen."

It's also worth remembering that immigrants are net contributors to the federal government's two most expensive entitlement programs—Medicare and Social Security—since they tend to arrive in the United States at the start of their optimal working years. Medicare and Social Security are pay-as-you-go programs. That means current tax payments are financing current benefits. Because some 70 percent of immigrants are between ages twenty and fifty-four (versus just half of the native population), and because 12 percent of natives are age sixty-five or older (compared to only 2 percent of immigrants), these foreign workers will pay some $5 trillion more in payroll taxes than they will receive in Social Security benefits. Never mind that these surplus payments more than offset any welfare benefits that most immigrants enjoy. The real outrage is that baby boomers like Lou Dobbs make a living vilifying these folks to boost ratings, when they should be throwing them a ticker tape parade for helping to keep America's two costliest "welfare" programs solvent.

Putting aside immigration's influence on the 1996 reforms, foreign nationals were never the bulk of welfare users to begin with, and the welfare "magnet" argument has always been far-fetched. There's evidence that some immigrants have abused the system, to be sure. In 1994, for example, Congress conducted a hearing on fraud in the SSI program that involved noncitizens using Southeast Asian middlemen to bring over their elderly parents to receive benefits. But the practice was not widespread, and the 1996 reforms closed the loophole that was being exploited. Even Harvard economist George Borjas, a Cuban immigrant who's made a name for himself advocating for less Latino immigration, concedes that the welfare magnet argument for sealing the border is anecdotal and weak. "[T]here exists the possibility that welfare attracts persons who otherwise would not have migrated to the United States," he writes in *Heaven's Door*, his influential 1999 book on immigration policy. "Although this is the magnetic effect that comes up most often in the immigration debate, it is also the one for which there is no empirical support. . . ."

Welfare use among unskilled immigrants is higher than among natives because those immigrants tend to have lower incomes and more of them are poor. Among those U.S. residents who are eligible to receive welfare, however, immigrants are not heavy users. Analyses of welfare use conducted by researchers at The Urban Institute have found that fewer than 1 percent of illegal immigrant households nationwide receive benefits for the program most commonly associated with welfare—Temporary Assistance for Needy Families—versus 5 percent of households headed by U.S. citizens.

A 2007 study of census data released by the Center on Budget and Policy Priorities also pokes holes in the welfare magnet theory. It found that, between 1995 and

2005—again, a period during which illegal immigration grew—the share of low-income, noncitizen immigrant children receiving Medicaid or State Children's Health Insurance Program (SCHIP) benefits fell from 36 percent to 30 percent. By comparison, participation in those programs among low-income native children over the same period—whether they lived in households headed by immigrants or native-born citizens—increased from 45 percent to 54 percent.

The public perception is that immigrants receive public benefits at higher rates than natives, but that's not what the data show. Overall, low-income immigrants have lower TANF, food stamp, and SSI use rates than citizens. That was true before welfare reform's enactment, and it remains the case today.

STATE AND LOCAL COSTS

It is not the federal government, however, that bears the fiscal brunt of immigration. That falls to states and localities, and some argue that even if the feds come out ahead, states with high immigrant populations are left holding the bag. It's true that the burden sharing is uneven, and states are right to complain that the feds don't do more to share their immigrant revenue surplus. In our federalist system, it's the states who pay most of the up-front costs of providing public services—the biggest items being K-12 schooling and health care—for poor immigrants.

Washington could and should do more to compensate these state and local governments. As Dan Griswold of the Cato Institute has pointed out, there's nothing stopping the federal government from transferring money to states to offset additional costs for emergency room health-care services and increased public school enrollment. Such a policy would have the virtue of addressing the problem without creating "any new programs or additional spending," says Griswold. "[I]t would simply reallocate government revenues in a way that more closely matched related spending."

Still, the significance of this state and local burden is regularly overstated by immigration skeptics. An oft-cited 1997 report by the National Research Council examined what immigrants were costing the Garden State and the Golden State and found that "the average native household bears an overall fiscal burden of $229 in New Jersey and $1,174 in California," the difference having mostly to do with the latter's "relatively more generous welfare programs." Nationally, the study found, immigrants were a short-term net drain on the average native household to the tune of $200, or a tiny 0.2 percent of GDP. And those results come from data that predate the 1996 welfare reforms, which means that today the burden is likely even less.

A more recent Winthrop Rockefeller Foundation report,

from 2007, on how Latino immigrants impact Arkansas's state coffers found that they "have a small but positive net fiscal impact on the Arkansas state budget." Taking into account both education and health care, immigrants "cost" the state $237 million in 2004 but made direct and indirect tax contributions of $257 million. Even more important, immigrant Arkansans generated some $3 billion in business revenues, in the process making significant contributions to the state's overall economic productivity and keeping it competitive in key industries.

According to the authors, *sans* immigrant labor "the output of the state's manufacturing industry would likely be lowered by about $1.4 billion—or about 8 percent of the industry's $16.2 billion total contribution to the gross state product in 2004." Immigrants also saved the state a bundle in manufacturing wages. It would have cost $95 million more for the same output without immigrants. Not only could those savings be passed on to consumers in the form of lower prices, but they also help keep Arkansas businesses competitive.

In 2006, the University of North Carolina (UNC) issued a similar report profiling that state's immigrant population. There, researchers found immigrants to be a small net cost ($61 million) to the state budget—estimated at $102 per Latino resident—though the authors cautioned that, for a proper understanding of the overall impact, the cost "must be seen in the broader context of the aggregate benefits Hispanics bring to the state's economy."

Like Arkansas's, North Carolina's economy is better off because of immigrants. By expanding the population—and thus the demand for housing, cars, clothes, refrigerators, washing machines, televisions, and countless other consumer goods and services—these newcomers expand markets and help business revenues grow. Imported human capital also translates into more economic output and cost competitiveness in important industries. According to the UNC study, without Hispanic immigrants North Carolina's construction industry output would almost certainly be much lower, and the state private sector would be paying nearly $2 billion more in wages. The state has also benefited from more trade with Latin America, which was responsible for some seventy thousand jobs and $231 million in state and local taxes in 2004.

What's happened in Arkansas and North Carolina is important because their immigrant populations are among the fastest-growing in the country. Arkansas ranked fourth nationwide in immigrant population growth between 1990 and 2000. Between 2000 and 2005, its Hispanic population grew by 48 percent, or faster than any other state in the United States. In North Carolina, Latinos accounted for more than a quarter of the population growth between 1990 and 2004. Between 1995 and 2004, 38 percent of these newcomers migrated from abroad, and 40 percent came from other parts of the United States.

More than half of Arkansas immigrants are here illegally, as are nearly half of North Carolina's. If importing large numbers of low-skill Latino immigrant "welfare cases" is bad news for a state's economic health, it would be manifest in these states. Instead, the opposite is true. Both states are experiencing economic boons and record-high immigration simultaneously, which is the story of much of the southeastern United States in recent years.

And if, as restrictionists insist, immigrants are coming here not to work but to take advantage of our "magnetic" social welfare programs, why are they flocking disproportionately to states that are so skimpy with benefits for the poor? Social welfare spending in Arkansas is among the lowest in the country. It's slightly higher in North Carolina but still well below the national average. The same holds true for other states that are experiencing big increases in immigrant populations, including South Carolina, Utah, Georgia, Arizona, Tennessee, Alabama, Indiana, Mississippi, Kansas, Nebraska, and Iowa.

There appears to be no correlation between generous state welfare benefits and growing immigrant populations. If Arkansas is the Scrooge of welfare benefits, California is closer to the Santa Claus. Yet it's the latter's immigrant population growth that's slowing. Latinos are economic migrants first and foremost. They settle where they do based primarily on the availability of employment. And once there, they help expand the economy and create more jobs. The United States is a magnet for people looking for work, not handouts.

California and Texas are the states with the most people. Serving as immigrant portals, they rank first and third (with New York in between) in the sizes of their foreign-born populations. California has by far the country's largest illegal alien population at 2.8 million (though the state's share of the nation's total has been falling), followed once again by Texas, which has half as many undocumented migrants. The experience of these two states is instructive, or should be, for anyone interested in facts about public benefits and immigrants, rather than emotion or populist rhetoric.

In what its authors describe as "the most detailed analysis to date of immigrants and their use of health services," a 2006 Rand Corporation study estimates that each year the United States spends "about $1.1 billion in federal, state, and local government funds on heath care for illegal immigrants aged 18–64." That works out to $11 per household.

Lou Dobbs informs his viewers that thousands of illegal alien lepers are scurrying across the Mexican border, infecting Americans and spiking health-care costs. But the Rand researchers found that nonelderly adult immigrants, both legal and illegal, made fewer visits to the hospital than their native-born counterparts. And the foreign-born—especially the undocumented—reported fewer health problems than natives. In 2000, illegal immigrants were 12 percent of Los Angeles County residents, yet received just 6 percent of total medical spending.

How to explain? "Most of the costs for undocumented immigrants' health care were covered by private insurance or out-of-pocket payments," according to the report, "but an estimated $204 million [out of $887 million] was for publicly supported services." Native residents, the study found, "were more likely to use publicly funded services than foreign-born residents." Imagine that.

Health-care costs are rising independently of immigration. Scapegoating the latest arrivals will hardly lower our medical bills and is highly misleading besides. Given that immigrants tend to be younger and healthier than natives, they're actually less likely to rack up large health bills. Recent immigrants from Mexico are also less inclined than most natives to use hospital emergency rooms, though you often hear claims to the contrary. A 2005 University of California at Los Angeles study found that fewer than 10 percent of Mexican aliens—legal and illegal—who'd been in the United States less than a decade reported using an emergency room, compared to 20 percent of white citizens. So much for the myth of freeloading illegals.

And then there's Texas, home to our second-largest illegal population. In 2006, the Texas comptroller, Carole Keeton Strayhorn, issued a report on how undocumented immigrants affect the state budget and economy. The first of its kind in Texas, according to Strayhorn, the study looked at gross state product, revenues generated, taxes paid, and the cost of state services. Education was the largest cost, while state-paid health care for illegals "was a small percentage of total health care spending." It found that illegal immigrants in Texas generate more taxes and revenue than the state spends on them.

What's more, the fiscal impact wasn't simply not negative; it was remarkably positive. Without immigrants—without *illegal* immigrants—Texas is worse off. The report found that "*the absence of the estimated 1.4 million undocumented immigrants in Texas in fiscal 2005 would have been a loss to our Gross State Product of $17.7 billion. Also, the Comptroller's office estimates that state revenues collected from undocumented immigrants exceed what the state spent on services, with the difference being $424.7 million*" (emphasis in the original).

Texas is a relatively low-levy state, one of only nine with no income tax. The taxes it does impose tend to be consumption based, which conservatives like because consumption taxes are more broad based (and thus, more fair) and don't punish savings and investment like steeply graduated income taxes do. But instead of advocating for more Texas-like state tax systems that would go a long way toward rendering this low-income immigrant/public benefits issue moot, and that are better in any case, some conservatives prefer to agitate for fewer immigrants. Principle takes a backseat.

And so it goes with health care. Health-care costs aren't what they are because of immigrants but because we have employer-provided health insurance. A third party rather than the patient is paying most of the medical tab. When people are spending other people's money, they tend to spend more of it, which drives up costs. We then exacerbate the situation by mandating what a health plan must cover and prohibiting employers from providing a bare-bones insurance option with a high deductible at a modest price. These regulations also result in more people without health insurance, since many employers opt not to insure their employees at all rather than offer an expensive plan that would force them to reduce wages.

These are problems, to be sure, but they are heath-care problems, not immigration problems. They are problems that would exist even if every foreign national in the country up and left tomorrow. The free-market solution to rising medical costs and emergency rooms full of uninsured patients isn't ramparting the Rio Grande. It's medical savings accounts and other reforms for low-income individuals who've been priced out of the market by special-interest regulations masquerading as consumer protections. It's ending "guaranteed issue" requirements that allow people to wait until they're sick to buy insurance, and "community rating" requirements that prevent insurers from charging different prices to different people based on age and health status. It's moving the entire U.S. health-care system more generally in a market-based direction.

The Texas study is a model for other states looking to determine the economic impact of immigration. Not only does it recognize that immigrants are a catalyst for economic growth, but it's also careful about how it identifies the immigrant population. A similar Colorado report overstated the health-care costs of illegal immigrants by including the health-care costs of many legal immigrants. The same Colorado study also inflated the costs of educating immigrants by assuming that all illegals between the ages of five and seventeen were in public schools, not accounting for the fact that some were enrolled in private schools and others did not attend school at all.

Strayhorn references a report by the nativist Federation for American Immigration Reform that stacks the deck by including as an illegal alien "cost" the education of their American-born children, who are, in fact, U.S. citizens—until a constitutional amendment says otherwise. That's significant because some two-thirds of the children of illegal immigrants, and 80 percent of the children of legal immigrants, are U.S. born. Such human capital expenditures, properly understood, are a net investment, and the children of immigrants—including Latinos—typically do better than their parents in terms of schooling and income. It's a strange logic that assumes American children are a fiscal burden to society.

ROBERT RECTOR AND ARITHMETIC

There's no credible research demonstrating that immigration imposes a large economic cost on the United States. The findings in smaller states like Arkansas and North

Carolina, or larger states like California and Texas, are not sui generis. They're the product of standard economic analyses that incorporate realistic assumptions. There is a cost component to low-skill immigration, to be sure, especially in border communities and states with large public benefits. But immigrants are also catalysts for economic growth. They increase the number of agents in the marketplace—the number of people who earn, spend, and invest—and thus the amount of economic activity. Any study of the fiscal impact of immigrants that leaves out these contributions is not telling the whole story.

Even if you accept the Borjas model that shows that low-skilled immigrants sometimes depress the pay of low-skill natives, it means they're also increasing profits, other things being equal. Greater profits tend to raise rates of return on investment, which leads to a larger supply of loanable funds, lower interest rates, and more capital formation. Nativists ignore these secondary and tertiary effects, preferring static-model half-truths to more dynamic assessments. But conservatives know better, or should.

Supply siders have for decades been critical of the way federal agencies like the Congressional Budget Office and the Joint Committee on Taxation estimated, or "scored," the effects of tax cuts on revenue without figuring in their effects on the overall economy. And rightly so. Under static modeling, for instance, if a state doubles its cigarette tax, it will double its revenue from that tax. But that doesn't take into account, as a dynamic model would, the fact that the tax increase will affect behavior. Some smokers, for example, may quit or smoke less. The tobacco taxes they previously paid would be lost to the state, offsetting some of the additional revenue anticipated by increasing the tax rate. Similarly, a tax cut might not result in a revenue reduction if it stimulates more economic activity.

The debate came to a head in the 1980s during the Reagan administration. Due to budget rules, it was difficult politically to advocate tax cuts because they represented revenue losses, according to static scoring. Conservatives became vocal proponents for a more dynamic analysis of the proposed Reagan tax cuts. The Gipper got his tax cuts and proved the static scorers wrong. The top tax rate in the United States fell from 70 percent in 1980 to 28 percent in 1988, while income tax revenues swelled by more than 54 percent. When President Bush halved capital gains taxes in 2003, the static models once again predicted disaster, yet another revenue surge ensued. Receipts in 2005 were the highest in more than twenty years.

When it comes to the economic impacts of immigration, however, some conservatives toss dynamism out the window. It doesn't matter if immigrants, who are both potential employees and potential customers, help expand the economy. Robert Rector, the welfare scholar at the free-market Heritage Foundation, has published a number of influential papers arguing that the measure of a Manuel is the difference between what he pays in taxes and receives in public benefits. Period. Rector maintains that low-skill immigrants are layabouts who "assimilate to welfare," generation after generation with no hope of upward mobility, and his reports and testimony before Congress in 2007 became grist for talk radio and cable news populists.

The *Wall Street Journal* editorial page picked apart Rector's arguments, as did free marketers like Daniel Griswold of the Cato Institute. Census data, among other indicators, show that immigrants significantly increase their earnings after arriving in the United States, which suggests they're assimilating to the workforce, not welfare. Even liberals can see this, and they didn't hesitate to critique Heritage's scare mongering by employing a dynamic approach to the readily available fiscal data. Ultimately, the think tank was hoisted by its own analytic petard.

But first, some background. Along with other conservative outfits like the National Center for Policy Analysis and the Institute for Policy Innovation, Heritage helped pioneer the use of dynamic analysis. Whether the issue was trade liberalization or tax policy, free-market conservatives regularly mocked economic studies that took into account only static impacts. "[No] matter how many times a 'static' analysis is disproved," Heritage Foundation president Ed Feulner once wrote, "Congress keeps doing business in the same wrongheaded way." When President Bush's 2007 budget proposal included a plan to create a Dynamic Analysis division inside the Treasury Department to assess how tax laws affect economic activity, William Beach, Heritage's top numbers cruncher, praised the move. "Inside the Beltway, this type of work is called 'dynamic analysis,'" Beach wrote in *BusinessWeek*. "Outside the Beltway, this is called 'economics.'"

Back in 1984, Heritage thought differently about immigration. That was the year it published an important paper by Julian Simon showing how poor immigrants help subsidize the country's costliest public benefits programs, Medicare and Social Security, by paying taxes for decades without ever receiving a check. A 1998 study by Beach also reported that Latino immigrants pay more into Social Security than they receive in their lifetime. A lot more. In 1997 dollars, he calculated, the typical Latino couple received nearly $350,000 less in lifetime benefits than it paid into the system.

This history hasn't been lost on Heritage's critics—liberal or conservative—in the recent debate over comprehensive immigration reform. But those on the political left in particular seemed to enjoy employing progrowth counterarguments to push back at the organization's newfound restrictionism. When Rector published a study in April 2007 arguing that low-skill immigrants are a net drain on the economy—and speculating that allowing any more such individuals into the United States "would dramatically increase the future fiscal burden to taxpayers"—it drew a pointed, supply-side response from the left-wing Immigration Policy Center (IPC).

Curiously absent from Rector's study, wrote IPC researchers Walter Ewing and Ben Johnson, was any discussion of the U.S. economy's high demand for low-skill labor. Apparently, it never occurred to Rector that immigrants might be incentivized by labor market forces rather than potential welfare benefits. The authors went on to chide Rector for his "narrow fiscal accounting" methods, which assume that if an immigrant's tax payments don't cover the cost of public services and benefits that he receives, it follows that the immigrant is a drain on the public fisc and the economy as a whole. But it doesn't follow.

"A comparison of the taxes that people pay and the public benefits and services they consume at a particular point in time does not measure the larger economic impact that they have through their consumer purchasing power and entrepreneurship, both of which create new jobs," wrote the authors, who would never be mistaken for Art Laffer. "Nor does it account for the upward economic mobility that many low-income families experience from generation to generation, particularly immigrant families."

Suffice it to say that if you're a right winger like Robert Rector, and you find yourself getting schooled on the economic facts of life by the likes of the Immigration Policy Center, you might need to revisit Friedrich Hayek, or at least reread *Wealth and Poverty*. Ewing and Johnson's takedown of a shoddy static economic analysis probably approximates anything the Heritage Foundation itself could have produced—and perhaps would have produced—if it hadn't, to the dismay of us free marketeers, decided to join the Dark Side on immigration.

AMERICA'S HARDEST WORKERS

The journalist Tamar Jacoby once wrote that "most foreigners, whether they arrive legally or illegally, come to the United States to work. Most do not come in the expectation of living on welfare." After all, says Jacoby, "if you're going to be unemployed, it's much better to be unemployed at home than in the United States. It's usually warmer at home and less expensive to live, and you are likely to be surrounded by a network of supportive family and friends."

Jacoby is spot-on, according to the economic data used to gauge an immigrant's intentions. The labor force participation rate, which measures the percent of the working-age population that is employed or seeking employment, is the strongest indication that immigrants come here to work and not to idle. Among foreign nationals generally, labor participation rates are higher than that of natives (69 percent versus 66 percent in 2006) and jobless rates are lower (4.0 percent versus 4.7 percent in 2006). This disparity only increases with respect to Hispanic males, who boast the highest labor-participation rate of any group in the country. Recent census figures put it at 88 percent for Mexican-born males, against 83 percent for their native counterparts. What about all those supposedly shiftless illegals who come here to "assimilate to welfare"? They have a labor force participation rate of 94 percent, and that's not a typo.

The Pew Hispanic Center published a study in 2006 that tracked migration flows back to 1990. The biggest factor affecting the rise and fall of border crossings was the state of the U.S. economy. Interestingly, the longer those immigrants are here, the harder they work. The unemployment rate for illegal aliens who arrived between 2000 and 2005 was 5.8 percent, compared with 4.1 percent for those arriving prior to 2000.

Among natives, low-skill black males have by far the lowest labor participation rates, and some opponents of immigration are quick to blame Latinos. There's no doubt some correlation, since it's these blacks who are most likely to compete for jobs with Mexicans. But given that black alienation from the workforce has not ebbed and flowed with Hispanic migration patterns but remained stubbornly consistent for decades, there's probably more to the story. When William Julius Wilson was writing about black nonattachment to the labor force twenty years ago, immigration was scarcely mentioned. He was primarily concerned with the deindustrialization of the U.S. economy, the lack of job training for blacks, and a hellish, self-perpetuating ghetto culture that encouraged criminal behavior and left too many black men not simply unemployed but unemployable.

The 1980s and 1990s saw two of the longest periods of sustained economic growth in U.S. history, yet the labor-force participation rates of less-educated young black men actually declined over that stretch. Black unemployment is nearly double the white rate and well above that of Hispanics, even though English-language skills alone should theoretically give blacks a major advantage with employers over Latino new arrivals. Nevertheless, those Latinos have displayed a greater willingness to accept and greater ability to retain low-skill jobs. By and large, black men aren't being shoved aside for these positions; the more likely explanation is that they're not interested in them. Black social pathology is a long and complex story. But Latino immigrants are not to blame.

If you're looking for a villain behind the black unemployment rate, try the welfare state. If welfare has served as a sort of settlement assistance program for immigrants who essentially come here to work, it has been a lure and a trap for the native poor. The black family survived slavery, Reconstruction, and Jim Crow, but the well-intentioned Great Society sounded its death knell. Daniel Patrick Moynihan was one of the first to notice this back in the late 1960s, when black male employment rates began to suffer. Difficult as it may be to fathom today, black participation in the labor force in the 1950s more or less matched that of whites. Today's discrepancy has less to do with immigrants than with government programs that inadvertently displaced black fathers as breadwinners. There's little evidence that the prospect of life on the dole drives low-skill immigration in the twenty-first century. But many of the jobs Mexicans fill are in fact available because the welfare state has made them less attractive to lower-skilled Americans.

It's indisputable that Latin American immigrants increase the ranks of the poor in the short run, just as previous waves of Italians, Irish, Poles, and Slavs did. All were labor migrants. Typically, they arrived poor and unskilled, taking jobs in mining, construction, and other industries. Mexicans are following this pattern. And the issue isn't their low socioeconomic status upon arrival so much as whether they remain that way for generations on end.

Normally, it's liberals who traffic in class-envy statistics, fretting about "income inequality," "stagnant wages," "rising poverty," "the disappearing middle class," and the plight of the "working poor." A 2004 *BusinessWeek* story was typical of this thinking. It noted that "one in four workers earns $18,800 a year or less," and went on to prescribe the usual left-wing remedies, including higher minimum wages and more unions. But free-market conservatives know that such income data is misleading. A third of those people are part-time workers and another third are under twenty-five. That leaves us with one-third of one-fourth—or roughly 8 percent of this subgroup—who are actually "working poor" in any long-term sense.

Poverty is transient for the overwhelming majority of Americans, so a snapshot of who's in the bottom fifth of income earners at any one point in time doesn't tell you much. Nearly 86 percent of tax filers in the bottom 20 percent in 1979 had exited that quintile by 1988. The corresponding mobility rates for the second-lowest, middle, second-highest, and highest quintiles are 71 percent, 67 percent, 62.5 percent and 35.3 percent, respectively. Overall, an absolute majority of the people in the bottom income quintile in 1975 have since also been in the top quintile.

All this mobility is one reason that Democratic attempts at class warfare are regularly rejected by most voters. Republicans, for their part, routinely chide the left for trying to play one earner against another. But when the subject turns to immigrants, conservatives can start to sound like John "Two Americas" Edwards. Robert Rector says we're "importing poverty," end of story. Journalist Heather Mac Donald says "we're importing a second underclass," "very, very low-skilled labor that's driving down wages." Mac Donald says that this is why "wages have been basically stagnant in low-skilled industries."

National Review and any number of restrictionist lawmakers in the GOP have made similar remarks. But what undermines these claims, whether they come from the left or the right, is the fact that it's difficult to work full-time and remain poor in the United States. Most people who are working are not poor. And most people who are poor are not working. We know from labor participation rates that low-skill immigrants are society's hardest workers. Which means that even if they arrive poor, they're not likely to stay that way.

Labor migrants are in search of a place where, given their skills, they can be more productive and earn more money. By heading north, a typical Mexican immigrant can nearly quadruple his hourly wage, and that's even adjusting for cost-of-living differences in the two countries. Some come to make a better life for themselves in America. Others come to make a better life for their families back home, where they plan to return eventually. The average Mexican worker sends home 41 percent of his pay, making remittances Mexico's second-largest source of external revenue, just behind oil exports.

But it's not all about maximizing income. Immigrants from less-developed countries also migrate to diversify risk and gain access to capital. High inflation, sagging wages, and failing crops might result in a decision by the male head of household to go north in search of employment, while his wife and children stay behind and work in the local economy. If the situation back home doesn't improve or turns worse, remittances can make up the difference. Similarly, capital and credit markets back home may be weak or nonexistent for a Mexican who wants to start a business, build a home, or pay medical bills. A trip to the United States to work for a period of time may be the answer.

Which is to say that there are many reasons for immigrants to head our way, and one of the least likely lures is welfare. Immigrants tend to be motivated people looking to better their situation, not looking for hand-outs. For your typical Latino immigrant, being unemployed in the United States is far more expensive than being unemployed back home. The fear of freeloaders is a legitimate concern, but it is vastly overblown with respect to these newcomers. If conservatives are worried about too many snouts at the trough—and if they're remotely interested in any sort of ideological consistency—they should be working to restrict welfare payments, not immigrants.

CHAPTER FOUR

★

ASSIMILATION:
THE NATIVISTS ARE RESTLESS

Whether behind the scenes or within the government itself, Linda Chavez has been fighting the good conservative fight for more than a quarter-century. She's a veteran of the Reagan White House and a former executive director of the U.S. Commission on Civil Rights. She's a FOX News political analyst, a nationally syndicated columnist, and head of the Center for Equal Opportunity, a think tank that promotes assimilation over multiculturalism and actively opposes affirmative action quotas and bilingualism. She's written extensively on organized labor, including the book, *Betrayal: How Union Bosses Shake Down Their Members and Corrupt American Politics*. She was the Republican candidate for U.S.

Senator from Maryland in 1986 and President George W. Bush's nominee for Secretary of Labor in 2001 before withdrawing her name from consideration.

Chavez was born and raised in the United States, though as the surname suggests she is of Hispanic heritage. Still, she doesn't hesitate to take on the liberal ethnic activists whose identity politics do far more harm than good for the people they claim to represent. You probably have to be a member of a racial or ethnic minority to appreciate fully the flak that someone like Chavez catches for casting her lot with the political right. Personal attacks—complete with pop psychoanalysis—are considered fair game, even in the mainstream media. If Antonin Scalia opposes racial preferences, he's simply wrong (and evil). If Linda Chavez opposes them, she's not only wrong but also an ethnic traitor. And "ungrateful." And "self-hating." And a "sellout." To be Chavez requires uncommon mettle, with a courage of convictions that can withstand relentless below-the-belt criticism for the sin of thinking independently. Chavez has always been up to the task, and movement conservatism is the better for her participation.

But none of that ideological capital counted for much after Chavez penned a column on immigration in the spring of 2007 that ruffled some right-wing feathers. The Senate was considering immigration-reform legislation, and the country was in the middle of a high-volume debate over its merits. In her column titled, "Latino Fear and Loathing," Chavez had the gall to suggest that racial and ethnic animus was informing the national discussion, particularly on talk radio, cable news, and conservative Web sites.

Never mind that race and ethnicity have *always* informed our immigration debates. When it comes to determining who can and can't come here, they have been front and center. Two hundred and fifty years ago, in writings that predate the nation's founding, Benjamin Franklin complained that German immigrants, whom he called "the most stupid of their nation," were too plentiful. "Why should Pennsylvania, founded by the English, become a Colony of Aliens," he wrote in 1751, "who will shortly be so numerous as to Germanize us instead of us Anglifying them, and will never adopt our Language and Customs?" The racial focus of the nation's first major anti-immigration law, the Chinese Exclusion Act of 1882, need hardly be argued. (The name notwithstanding, the Alien and Sedition Acts of 1798 were less about restricting immigration than about Federalist attempts to muzzle political opponents.) Early twentieth-century eugenicists like Madison Grant and Harry Laughlin, who heavily influenced the Immigration Act of 1924, went so far as to present "scientific" data classifying Southern and Eastern Europeans as different (and inferior) races in order to oppose their entry to the United States. Even the 1965 Immigration and Nationality Act, which repealed the 1924 national-origin quotas and ended Asian exclusion policies, was viewed as a piece of civil rights legislation, given that it came out of a period when the United States was attempting to end centuries of legalized discrimination against blacks.

So when Chavez wrote in her column that "some people just don't like Mexicans—or anyone else from south of the border," she wasn't identifying a new phenomenon in American policy debates. She could point to well over 250 years of New World nativism to buttress her argument. Put another way, if race and ethnicity *weren't* factors in the most recent immigration fight, it might well be the first time in U.S. history that that was the case. Chavez's column continued, "They think Latinos are freeloaders and welfare cheats who are too lazy to learn English. They think Latinos have too many babies, and that Latino kids will dumb down our schools. They think Latinos are dirty, diseased, indolent, and more prone to criminal behavior. They think Latinos are just too different from us ever to become real Americans." Chavez said that a minority of the American public held these views, but among them were a "fair number of Republican members of Congress, almost all influential conservative talk radio hosts, some cable news anchors—most prominently, Lou Dobbs—and a handful of public policy 'experts' at organizations such as the Center for Immigration Studies, the Federation for American Immigration Reform, NumbersUSA, in addition to fringe groups like The Minutemen."

National Review was not among those named by Chavez, though it fit the profile. The magazine and its Web site have thundered against immigration on "cultural" grounds for years via writers such as David Frum, John O'Sullivan, Mark Krikorian, John Derbyshire, Peter Brimelow, and Samuel

Francis. Frum, O'Sullivan, Derbyshire, and Brimelow, are themselves beneficiaries of our open border policies but want to construct walls around their adopted homeland and raise the drawbridge. *National Review* has also run political cartoons that demean Latinos, like the one that appeared in its July 9, 2007, issue. It shows a woman standing next to a man who has just erected a large billboard on the Mexican border that reads SHIRT AND SHOES REQUIRED. The man then turns, hammer in hand, to the woman and says, "This way, maybe we'll get a better class of illegal alien."

When the Chavez column appeared, *National Review* editors had a fit. Contributing editor Mark Levin called the piece "malignant" and "shameful." He said it was Chavez— not radio personalities like Laura Ingraham, television personalities like Lou Dobbs, and politicians like Tom Tancredo—who had "reduce[d] this debate to the most base level." Levin said, "This issue isn't about any particular race or group of people, and any honest observer knows it." Another contributing editor, John Derbyshire, who proudly calls himself a "racist" and a "homophobe," defended Dobbs's nightly rants against Mexican immigrants. The CNN anchor is married to a woman "of Mexican ancestry," noted Derbyshire, and ipso facto incapable of anti-Hispanic bias. I'm sure some of Derbyshire's best friends are black homosexuals.

Senior editor Ramesh Ponnuru went furthest of all, willfully distorting Chavez's central argument by claiming that she thinks "anyone who disagrees with her about immigration policy is a racist." And in a display of remarkable self-regard, even for Ponnuru, he called on conservatives everywhere to disassociate themselves from Chavez, melodramatically declaring, "I will never trust her judgment again."

To its credit the magazine's Web site invited Chavez to expand on her original column, and she used the opportunity to focus on the commentary of Heather Mac Donald in particular. Mac Donald is a highly respected journalist based at the Manhattan Institute who has written extensively on Hispanic culture and the grave danger it poses, in her view, to the future of America's Anglo-Protestant social fabric. Over the years, she has written thoughtfully and persuasively on any number of topics, but when she turns her attention to Latino immigration her commentaries ooze vitriol and seem intended more to frighten and demean than inform.

As an example, Chavez cited an essay by Mac Donald mockingly titled, "Hispanic Family Values?" Says Chavez: "Mac Donald's article is a litany of dysfunction and pathology among Hispanics—mothers pimping their own daughters, incest, drugs, ubiquitous illegitimacy, and welfare dependence." Elsewhere, Mac Donald has employed reckless generalizations, claiming that Latinos are culturally averse to marriage, congenital violent criminals, and that "cutting school is something of a tradition among Hispanics." On occasion, she feels the need to dehumanize illegal aliens entirely. In one article she referenced a newspaper headline that read, "Patients, Fearing INS Raids, Don't Seek Health

Care," and then wrote, sarcastically, "And what exactly is wrong with that?"

Chavez argued that it's "dangerous to win the immigration debate by stirring up racial or ethnic animosities by playing to the prejudices of that small group of Americans who are motivated by racism and nativism." And she said there's more than enough blame to go around. "I don't for a minute believe that the Left isn't guilty of similar sins; I've made a career of attacking the Left when it veered into anti-Americanism or promoting racial divisions. But I expect more from my fellow conservatives."

DIGESTING WHAT WE'VE EATEN

Mac Donald's central concern is that Latinos, for various reasons, are either incapable of assimilation or not interested in trying. And while she overstates her case, and is needlessly bellicose in presenting it, her view is hardly unique or original. As Benjamin Franklin demonstrated, the fear that newcomers will dilute the essential character of the country—that immigrants will change America more than America will change immigrants—is as old as the country itself.

Calls for an immigration moratorium or "time-out" are also old hat. In the congressional debate over the Immigration Act of 1924, Senator Ellison DuRant Smith argued that the country already had enough foreigners. "I think we have sufficient stock in America now for us to shut the door, Americanize what we have, and save the resources of America for the natural increase of our population." It's worth noting that at the time of Smith's floor speech—which invoked the theories of Madison Grant to argue that lower levels of immigration were needed to preserve America's Anglo-Saxon culture—the Chinese Exclusion Act was already in effect, and Congress had passed severe restrictions on Southern and Eastern European immigration only three years earlier, in the Emergency Quota Act of 1921. Nevertheless, Smith felt too much foreign riffraff was still washing ashore.

"Thank God we have in America perhaps the largest percentage of any country in the world of the pure, unadulterated Anglo-Saxon stock," said Smith. "It is for the preservation of that splendid stock that has characterized us that I would make this [country] not an asylum for the oppressed of all countries, but a country to assimilate and perfect that splendid type of manhood that has made America the foremost Nation in her progress and her power."

Senator Smith was a silver-tongued segregationist from South Carolina, a Democrat who defended the Southern way of life until his death in 1944. But on immigration he spoke for most of the Senate; the 1924 act passed with only six dissenting votes. And if you listen closely to today's immigration debate, Smith's voice can still be heard, and not just among Internet cranks and talk radio Know-Nothings.

Plenty of fair-minded Americans, of all races and ethnicities, fear that we are not assimilating Latino aliens as fast as they are entering the country through Mexico. *Wall Street Journal* columnist Peggy Noonan wants the border closed "to give the latest wave of immigrants time to become Americans" and "time to absorb our meaning and history and traditions." In recent decades, she says, the country has "experienced the biggest wave of immigrants since the great wave of 1880–1920. And we've never stopped to absorb it. We have never stopped to digest what we've eaten." Many Americans, says Noonan, "want a pause, a stopping of the flow, a time for the new ones to settle down and settle in."

U.S. academics who favor less immigration from Latin America have also picked up on this theme. Samuel Huntington's *Who Are We?* and Victor Davis Hanson's *Mexifornia*, to cite two better-known examples, are both afflicted by the assimilation blues. Hanson, a classicist at California's Fresno State, says Latinos display a "stubborn resistance" to our culture and that the old Americanization model isn't working efficiently for the lion's share of these newcomers. He cites the "sheer numbers of Mexican people who speak poor English, show few professional skills, and are overrepresented in our jails."

Huntington, a Harvard political scientist, says European migrants a century ago "modified and enriched"

America, but today's Latino influx presents "a serious challenge to America's traditional identity." Mexican immigration, he warns, "is leading toward the demographic reconquista of areas Americans took from Mexico by force in the 1830s and 1840s." Latino immigration, says the professor, "poses a fundamental question: will the United States remain a country with a single national language and a core Anglo-Protestant culture?"

The real question, however, is whether these fears are well founded. Do the facts regarding today's newcomers square with the popular beliefs and widely held assumptions? For ratings-driven television and radio people, or myopic politicians out to demagogue an issue, or opinion journalists straining to be provocative, perception and reality are often one and the same. Playing up divisions and piling on can be an end to itself, regardless of whether the exercise enlightens the public and moves the debate forward. Again, to paraphrase the proverb, there's nothing exactly new here. But opponents of immigration have turned ignoring context, historical or otherwise, into something of a virtue, and nowhere is this more evident than in discussions of whether the latest arrivals are assimilating.

The claim, romanticized by Father Time and Tinseltown, is that prior Asian and European immigrants, from the Poles and the Jews to the Irish, Italians, and Chinese, pretty much checked their ethnic identities at Ellis Island and adopted American culture in no time at all. But Mexicans, we're told, are totally different, sui generis even.

Hanson writes that the traditional homesick immigrant was "barricaded in his new homeland by thousands of miles of ocean, with little hope of returning to the Old Country every few months, and thus had to deal with Americans." For the Mexican campesino, by contrast, "the Rio Grande is no ocean, but a trickle easily crossed by a drive over a tiny bridge." Huntington worries that too many are coming too fast, noting that in the 1990s Mexicans were "over one half of the Latin American immigrants to the United States, and Latin American immigrants were about one half the total immigrants to the continental United States between 1970 and 2000."

Pat Buchanan, to no one's surprise, is also deeply concerned about this slow but steady browning of America. "Mexicans not only come from another culture, but millions are of another race," he says, though Pitchfork Pat probably takes some comfort in knowing that at least they're not Jewish. Asian and European immigrants might have settled in to ethnic enclaves replete with stores and restaurants where people could speak their native tongue, but some see menace among Mexicans who do the same. "A spirit of separatism, nationalism, and irredentism is alive in the barrios," says Buchanan. He's also worried that these immigrants present a physical danger to U.S. natives. If for no other reason, in his view, Latino immigrants should be deported en masse because, he claims, they have a general contempt for the law and are exposing natives to tuberculosis, leprosy, and other Third World diseases. "The first duty of government is to protect its citizens," he writes in *State of Emergency: The Third World Invasion and Conquest of America*. "By allowing at least 12 million illegal aliens to remain in this country, among whom rates of crime and infectious and contagious diseases are far higher than among Americans, the Unites States government fails in its first duty."

THE PETER PAN FALLACY

If anything, nativists of old like Senator Ellison Smith had more reason to complain than we do. Back then, immigrant arrivals were much more numerous relative to the size of the U.S. population. In the 1990s, legal and illegal immigration from Mexico numbered an estimated 4.2 million, or 1.5 immigrants per 1,000 U.S. residents each year. By comparison, Dan Griswold of the Cato Institute has noted that in the midnineteenth century the United States absorbed an average of 3.6 Irish immigrants per 1,000 U.S. residents annually—more than double the current flow of Mexicans. For fifty years, from 1840 to 1890, the rate of German immigration was greater in every decade than the current flow of Mexicans. And from 1901 to 1910, Russian, Italian, and Austro-Hungarian immigration each surpassed the current rate of Mexican immigration.

Like today's Mexicans, the majority of those Southern and Eastern European labor migrants arrived poor and unskilled. They worked in industry, mining, and the building trades. Early on, they were employed as stable hands, lumbermen, dock workers, ditch diggers, and in other arduous jobs Americans didn't want. The men built canals and found work on railroads. The women toiled as domestics. They spoke foreign languages and settled in overcrowded, ethnically distinct ghettos where poverty and crime were pronounced.

Those immigrants didn't check their cultural baggage at Ellis Island, and that didn't go unnoticed by the natives. Ulster migrants were presented in the press as dim-witted drunks and whoremongers who were filling up the jails and asylums. They were also seen as dirty and diseased. Prior to large-scale Irish immigration in the mid-1800s, cholera cases were rare in American cities. After the Irish arrived, cholera epidemics swept through the neighborhoods in Boston and Philadelphia where they had settled. An outbreak in Boston in 1849 killed hundreds, and more than two-thirds of the fatalities were among the Irish. You can guess who the natives blamed.

By the second half of the nineteenth century, Italy had one of the highest illiteracy rates in Europe—62 percent in 1871. In response, the country passed a law in 1877 that made formal education compulsory for Italian children. In the Mezzogiorno, or Southern Italy, where more than 80 percent of Italian Americans trace their ancestry, illiteracy rates were even higher than the national average, and riots ensued after the law was enacted. The violent reaction reflected a cultural hostility to formal education. Lower-class Italians valued work over school and didn't trust the state authorities. Nearly 4 million Italians immigrated to the United States between 1880 and 1914, and those attitudes toward education came with them. Italian children subsequently struggled in schools, when they bothered to go at all. In 1910, according to the political historian Michael Barone, only 31 percent of Italian immigrants between fourteen and eighteen were enrolled in school, versus 48 percent for the Irish and 56 percent for the Jews. "Boys were encouraged to work as soon as possible, to bring money into the family," says Barone. To paraphrase Heather Mac Donald, cutting school was something of a tradition among Italians.

The Irish and Italian experiences were the rule, not the exception. Life in America was hard, and many weren't up for it. Even though "thousands of miles of ocean" separated them from their native lands, labor economist Michael Piore found that one-third of these European newcomers returned home in the period leading up to World War I. As with Mexicans today, some came, discovered that the streets weren't gilded, and left.

But of course the majority of those impoverished, poorly educated, and unskilled people decided to tough it out and make a better life for themselves and their families. And although there were many more such immigrants, relative to the size of nineteenth-century America, than we have today, the country (and the economy) eventually absorbed them. It didn't happen overnight, but it did happen, despite fears at the time that those folks were just too foreign. The doomsayers were wrong, and the United States became richer and stronger by ignoring them. Southern and Eastern Europeans eventually became as educated as other Americans, and as well represented in occupations requiring formal education.

Yes, it's true that Mexican immigrants are distinguished from prior immigrants groups by the fact that their homeland abuts the United States. But the significance of this distinction is often overstated. Keep in mind that the Mexican side of the border is mostly uninhabited. America-bound migrants tend to come from much farther south. Raul Hernandez-Coss of the World Bank traced the flow of remittances from different parts of the United States to different parts of Mexico, which mirror the migration flows from south to north. What he found is that Mexican emigrants are often traveling thousands of miles to seek work in the United States. The Latino immigrants you find in Omaha, Chicago, and Seattle, for example, typically hail from the rural Mexican state of Michoacán, which is just east of Mexico City, the capital. Michoacán is more than fifteen hundred miles from Chicago and some two thousand miles from Seattle. Mexican immigrants in Boston tend to come from the Mexican state of Jalisco, a little farther north, and those in New York come from Puebla, a state that is south of the capital and more than two thousand miles away. Let's just say these folks aren't any more likely to pop back home for weekend visits than were their European and Asian immigrant forbears.

It's also tempting to exaggerate the permanence of immigration from Latin America, but we shouldn't. Just because we see high numbers coming today doesn't mean they will continue coming tomorrow and the next day. In fact, we already may have passed the high-water mark for illegal immigration from our main "sending country," Mexico. Demographic trends south of the border show that the size of the young adult Mexican cohort, from which most immigrants are drawn, is declining. Mexico's population growth rate has dropped by more than 50 percent during the past five decades, from 3 percent in 1960 to 1.3 percent today. By 2050 the rate will be negative, according to United Nations forecasts. Indeed, the population growth rate in Mexico today is only slightly higher than Canada's. Just twenty-five years ago, Mexico had a population growth rate that was more than double that of our neighbor to the north.

Youth unemployment has also fallen as the Mexican economy has continued to expand, decreasing the likelihood of people heading north in search of employment. According to a Pew Hispanic Center study, the share of first-generation immigrants in the U.S. Latino population is on track to drop from about 40 percent in 2000 to closer to a third by 2020.

The political scientist Michael Barone says the Puerto Rican experience also suggests that Mexican immigration will taper off sooner rather than later. "In the 1950's of 'West Side Story,' it seemed that Puerto Rican immigrants would take over New York City," he wrote in *The Wall Street Journal*. "There were no barriers to that migration: Puerto Ricans are U.S. citizens and there were cheap flights from San Juan to New York. But around 1961, when per capital incomes in Puerto Rico reached about 35% of the U.S. average, net migration from Puerto Rico tapered off to zero, where it has remained ever since." Barone allows that incomes in Mexico are still well below that level, but adds, "at some point immigration from Mexico and other parts of Latin America will likely fall, as immigration from Germany and Britain and Ireland fell in the late nineteenth century as those countries' economies grew."

The traditional indicators of American assimilation include English use, poverty rates, education, and homeownership, and the worry is that Hispanic newcomers are lagging in all four measures. To the extent that it's true, it fits the historical pattern. The issue here is whether the Latino lag in acculturation and socioeconomic progress just seems worse than it really is due to the volume of Mexican immigration in recent decades. Immigration from all of Latin America totaled 3 million between 1981 and 1990. Immigration from Mexico alone totaled more than 4 million in the 1990s. Those kinds of numbers can and do produce an illusion of nonadvancement.

That's why it's important to remember, when considering "averages," that *Latino migration is ongoing.* The public is fed a lot of snapshot data on English-language skills and high school dropout rates, but they are of little use in measuring assimilation. What we really want to know is how immigrants are faring *over time*, and only longitudinal studies can provide that information. As Michael Barone writes in *The New Americans*, "The statistics showing that the average Latino has only slightly improved mastery of English, education levels, and incomes are actually evidence of substantial gains." How so? Because "overall statistics that average in huge numbers of new arrivals mask the progress that preexisting immigrants have made."

In *Immigrants and Boomers*, Dowell Myers expands on this point, calling it the Peter Pan fallacy. Many observers, consciously or not, embrace a misconception that immigrants never change and retain all the characteristics they possessed on arrival. "Many of us assume, unwittingly, that immigrants are like Peter Pan," says Myers, "forever frozen in their status as newcomers, never aging, never advancing economically, and never assimilating." In this naive view, he says, "the mounting numbers of foreign-born residents imply that our nation is becoming dominated by growing numbers of people who perpetually resemble newcomers." Myers goes on to present evidence that real progress is being made by Latinos. Granted, progress is slower in some areas, such as the education level of adult immigrants, and faster in others, such as income and homeownership rates. But there is no doubt that both assimilation and upward mobility are occurring over time.

Europeans Then, Latin Americans Now

Linguistic assimilation is key, not least because it amounts to a job skill that can increase earnings. And while restrictionists claim otherwise, there's simply no evidence that Latinos are rejecting English. "The model that we have from the European experience," sociologist Richard Alba told me in an interview, "is that the children of immigrants born in the U.S. grow up in homes where they learn, to some extent, the mother tongue. They understand it and may speak it, but they prefer English. And when they grow up, they establish homes where English is the dominant language."

According to 2005 census data, just one-third of immigrants who are in the country for less than a decade speak English well, but that fraction climbs to nearly three-quarters for those here thirty years or more. There may be more bilingualism today among the children of immigrants, but there's no indication that Spanish is dominant in the second generation. The 2000 census found that 91 percent of the children and 97 percent of the grandchildren of Mexican immigrants spoke English well. Nor are there signs, bilingual-education advocates notwithstanding, that immigrant parents *want* their children speaking Spanish. A 2002 Pew Hispanic Center/Kaiser Foundation survey found that 89 percent of Latinos "believe immigrants need to learn to speak English to succeed in the United States."

Longitudinal analyses also reveal that homeownership is up and poverty is down among the Latino immigrants.

Using as his sample California, which has the country's largest concentration of Mexican foreign nationals, Myers notes that 16 percent of Latinos arriving in the Golden State in the 1970s owned homes by 1980. But more than 33 percent owned homes by 1990, and over half by 2000. The average rate of homeownership nationally was just over 66 percent in 2000.

The 2000 census found that the foreign-born poverty rate had fallen slightly, to 19.1 percent from 19.8 percent in 1990. Myers reports that this small decrease was not due to an influx of more prosperous immigrant groups, such as Asians. The disaggregated data show that poverty fell among Latinos and Asians alike. Nor can it be attributed to a temporary upturn in the economy, since the economic conditions measured in the 1990 and 2000 censuses were similar. Again using as his sample California, Myers found that poverty reversal was directly attributable to the maturing of California's immigrant population. Longer-residing immigrants generally experience substantial improvements in poverty, but in the past those gains were overshadowed by the increasing numbers of newcomers. He explains: "Now that the longer-settled immigrants are beginning to outweigh the newcomers in number, the force of upward mobility is no longer being offset by the relatively high poverty of newcomers, and the total poverty rate of the foreign-born has turned around."

Myers is hardly the only social scientist to notice Latino upward mobility, and California isn't the only place it's happening. In a definitive longitudinal study in the 1990s, sociologists Alejandro Portes and Ruben Rumbaut found substantial second-generation progress among Latinos in Miami and Fort Lauderdale as well. Nationwide cross-generational studies show the same results. In 2006, economist James Smith of the RAND Corporation found that successive generations of Latinos have experienced significant improvements in wages relative both to their fathers and grandfathers and to the native whites with whom they compete for jobs. And Roger Waldinger and Renee Reichl, two UCLA social scientists, found that while first-generation Mexican men earned just half as much as white natives in 2000, the second generation had upped their earnings to three-quarters of their Anglo counterparts.

Yes, Latino immigrants are trailing economically. That's no surprise. In his book, *Italians Then, Mexicans Now*, economist Joel Perlmann says that earlier European immigrants "were at least as concentrated as the Mexicans of today in low-skill work, and at least as over-concentrated there relative to native whites—and this is also true if we restrict attention to those who are not working in agriculture." Perlmann is not convinced by those who claim that the income gap today between Mexicans and natives can't be compared to the earlier European immigrant experience. Harvard's Christopher Jencks, for example, has said that one reason "assimilation . . . proceeded quickly in the past was because the economic gap between immigrants and natives was far smaller than today's folklore suggests. Most immigrants were poor, but so were most natives."

Not so fast, says Perlmann. Jencks has oversimplified the historical record. Over time, wage inequality fluctuated for the millions of low-skill foreigners who arrived between the 1880s and the 1920s. Thanks to two world wars, the Roaring Twenties, and the Great Depression, among other shocks to our labor markets, the economic well-being of immigrants varied from decade to decade. In 1910, European immigrants were averaging 50 percent to 60 percent of the native white mean wage. By 1920, their wages had risen, relative to natives, by about 10 percentage points, but by 1940 they were back to 1920 levels, only to rise again by 1950.

Large numbers of Mexicans began arriving in the 1970s, and Perlmann found that, contrary to Jencks's implication, they did not start out as far below the native whites as did Southern and Eastern Europeans in 1910. "In terms of relative well-being," says Perlmann, "the 1970 Mexicans were probably comparable to the 1920 [European immigrants]— notwithstanding (we should note in passing) that many of the Mexicans but virtually none of the [European immigrants] arrived as undocumented workers and that that status certainly takes a toll on wage prospects." By 2000, the wage gap for Mexicans had widened to about where it was for Europeans in 1910, which is worrisome but not—and this is the point—unprecedented. As Perlmann summarizes, the United States may indeed need to reform its immigration policy, "but not because of a supposed radical change in the relative wage status of labor migrants in 1910 and 2000."

ALL LATINOS AREN'T IMMIGRANTS

A bigger concern is education, though here, too, context is important. The correlation between higher levels of education and higher paychecks has never been stronger than it is today. Apprenticeships and other types of on-the-job training also tend to increase earnings, but education is the safest bet. In 2003 the average full-time worker in the United States with a four-year college degree earned $49,900, 62 percent more than someone with a high school diploma and 131 percent more than someone who never completed high school. Just finishing twelfth grade can push a worker's annual earnings more than 40 percent above someone who doesn't.

Among first-generation Mexican immigrants, 59 percent lack a high school degree. The good news is that the number falls dramatically in subsequent generations. According to 2004 census data, only 17 percent of the children of Mexican immigrants don't earn diplomas. The bad news is that very few go on to earn a college degree. The percentage of second-generation Mexicans who do grew from 3.2 percent in 1970 to 14.1 percent in 2004. But the corresponding increases among native whites possessing college degrees (from 11.8 percent to 31.7 percent) and among the total U.S. population (10.2 percent to 29.8 percent) means that Mexicans in effect have been *losing* ground.

A college education is far more common in 2004 than it was in 1970 among almost all groups except Mexican immigrants, explain sociologists Roger Waldinger and Renee Reichl in *Securing the Future*. And because the economy continues to put a premium on education, these low levels of college completion will almost certainly depress the earnings of second-generation Mexicans. The concern is echoed in a 2006 National Research Council report. On the one hand, rising numbers of Hispanic young people will slow the nation's overall population aging and can partially offset the growing burden of dependency produced by an aging majority. But the study goes on to say that their success in doing so "depends on the level of their earnings, which in turn depends on their education and acquisition of job-rated skills."

It's also important to keep in mind that all Latinos aren't immigrants, an obvious point that's conveniently forgotten among those trying to portray Hispanics in the worst possible light. For example, school completion rate data for Hispanics that don't disaggregate for the foreign born inevitably will overstate the achievement of immigrants and understate it for their U.S.-born children. Why? Because half of all adult Latinos in the country are foreign born, and more than half of the Mexicans who comprise most of the foreign-born population never completed high school.

When social conservatives cite Hispanic school dropout rates and teen pregnancy figures, the implication is that the dysfunctions of the inner-city black underclass can automatically be projected onto Mexican immigrants. But that's not necessarily the case. First-generation Mexicans may be the group least likely to be in school, but they are also the group most likely to be working; more than 81 percent of the men not in school hold a job. By contrast, note Waldinger and Reichl, "out-of-school African Americans appear the least likely to have moved from school to a job." What's more, "the employment rate of second-generation Mexican men is close to white men and diverges widely from that of African American men, among whom there is the weakest attachment to work."

Similarly, high teen pregnancy rates among Mexicans, while certainly troublesome in the abstract, should be put in perspective. If the black underclass is our frame of reference, we link out-of-wedlock births to single-parent homes and idle young men who sire children that they don't raise and don't provide for. That may be the black inner-city scenario, but by and large that's not what's going on among Mexican immigrants. High teen pregnancy rates notwithstanding, 80 percent of Mexican-American children are raised in two-parent families. Mexican women usually end up marrying the father of their children, which is not the case among blacks. As Chavez explains, "Hispanic marriage rates are nearly identical to those of non-Hispanic whites; 77 percent of Hispanic women will marry by age 30, compared to 81 percent of non-Hispanic whites, and they are no more likely to divorce."

DEPORT THE MULTICULTURALISTS

A couple of years ago, Boston College political scientist Peter Skerry penned an essay for *The Wilson Quarterly* on the history of the Statue of Liberty as a symbol of welcome to immigrants. Drawing on the work of historian John Higham, he explained how the statue originally had nothing to do with immigration. A gift from France to commemorate the centennial of our war for independence, Lady Liberty "was intended as a beacon of hope to those struggling for liberty in their own lands, not as a welcome light for those seeking liberty here," wrote Skerry. But symbols are mutable, and it didn't take long for the copper icon's transformation to occur, helped along by the Emma Lazarus sonnet it inspired.

However, today's immigration debate, like others in the past, is still very much about what the Statue of Liberty originally stood for: certain ideals and values. As Skerry puts it:

> Liberty was depicted as a woman whose austere, classical demeanor was meant to suggest the universality of America's founding ideals. These were underscored by the tablets of law that she cradles in one arm, and

the torch she holds high with the other. And with her back to New York, Liberty strides oceanward, sending her light out into the world.

Assimilation is less about immigrants adopting our culture than about immigrants adopting our values. And America has been uniquely successful in this regard. Canada has utterly failed to bridge its linguistic divide. French Canadians in Quebec aren't just pro–French language but also anti-English. The United States has as many French Canadians as does Canada, and a large percentage of them live in New England, yet there has been no such tension on this side of the border.

The British haven't been particularly adept at assimilation, either. Their approach has been to encourage a sort of permanent heterogeneous status for newcomers, with an emphasis on tolerance and respect but no real expectation that immigrants melt in. On the Continent, Western European countries like Germany, Italy, and Spain make no pretenses. They are truly ethnic societies where any ethnic divergence stands out. Given its history, Germany is careful about protecting civil liberties and has worked hard to banish any vestige of outright racial or ethnic discrimination. But as any Turk living there today will tell you, you're either German or you're not. Just like you're either Polish or not, Czech or not, and Italian or not. Even in Scandinavia, where political correctness is even more strenuous than in Germany, you're either Swedish or you aren't.

France at least gives lip service to the notion of accepting all newcomers as French. And it even has a national slogan—*"Liberté, égalité, fraternité, ou la mort!"*—that stresses ideals over ethnicity. But today that's mostly an elite conception. In practice, the motto is at odds with deep-seated cultural and ethnic habits, as demonstrated most recently by the Muslim riots of 2005, the country's worst since 1968.

The key to the success of the U.S. assimilation model, says Peter Salins, a senior fellow at the Manhattan Institute, is that "we put so much more stress on shared values rather than shared cultures." In an interview, Salins explained that immigrants find America's values and ideals as attractive as its economic opportunities. Yes, they come here to get rich, but it's more than that. It's also our value framework, with its emphasis on individual initiative and individual opportunity. Foreigners like the fact that you can make more money *because* you are hard-working or diligent or clever.

Salins says the other major value component is our civic institutions. We're the land of liberty and democracy. Here, people can say what they want, be what they want, do what they want. These are attractive values. And Americans are much more concerned about people sharing their values than sharing their cultural artifacts.

If American culture is under assault today, it's not from immigrants who aren't assimilating but from modern elites who reject the concept of assimilation. In *Who Are We?*, Samuel Huntington works from a definition of culture that is both broad and specific. Culture, he writes, refers to "a people's language, religious beliefs, social and political values, assumptions as to what is right and wrong, appropriate and inappropriate, and to the objective institutions and behavior pattern that reflect these subjective elements."

Key elements of America's Anglo-Protestant culture, he says, "include: the English language; Christianity; religious commitment; English concepts of the rule of law, the responsibility of rulers, and the rights of individuals; dissenting Protestant values of individualism, the work ethic, and the belief that humans have the ability and the duty to try to create a heaven on earth, a 'city on a hill.'"

Nothing indicates that today's immigrants, like those who came before them, don't share Huntington's commitment to those ideals. But there's plenty of evidence that those ideals make many of the professor's colleagues sick to their stomachs. For multiculturalists, assimilation is a dirty word that elicits not just indifference but outright hostility. Some don't want to judge one culture as superior or inferior to another, the type of relativism that Allan Bloom described so eloquently in *The Closing of the American Mind*. They espouse a kind of values-neutral belief system. If some societies believe in genital mutilation or keeping women uneducated and covered in a burka, who are we to judge?

But other multicultural elites, who dominate the academy, reject the assimilationist paradigm outright on the grounds that the United States hasn't always lived up to its stated ideals. Americans slaughtered Indians and enslaved blacks, goes the argument, and this wicked history means they have no right to impose a value system on others.

In other words, conservatives who want to seal the border because the liberal elites have taken over are directing their wrath at the wrong people. The problem isn't the immigrants, it's the elites and their multiculturalist predilections who want to turn America into a loose federation of ethnic groups. Conservatives are right to complain about bilingual education advocacy, anti-American Chicano studies professors, Spanish-language ballots, ethnically gerrymandered voting districts, La Raza's big government agenda, and so forth. But these problems weren't created by the women changing the linen at your hotel, or the men building homes in your neighborhood.

Keep the immigrants. Deport the Columbia faculty.

For all the loud talk of late, the American public seems not to have lost confidence in the melting pot. If it had, you'd know it. There would be "English-only" signs and militarized border zones. There would be ubiquitous police checkpoints and far-right political parties like France's National Front. Michelle Malkin would be considered a serious pundit, not Ann Coulter without the nuance.

Of course, there is some bigotry and stupidity out there, which we'll always have. But when people really believe they can't live another day with other kinds of people, they don't send e-mails to *The O'Reilly Factor*. They engage in ethnic warfare. You get the Serbs and the Croats in the Balkans, the Hindus and the Muslims in India, the Hutus and the

Tutsis in Rwanda. What we have in America is periodic grumpiness, short-lived sniffing about the most recent arrivals, a vague and ambivalent disdain that doesn't settle too deeply into the psyche. Americans still believe that our assimilationist model is working, even if the elites on the left and right who claim to speak on their behalf do not.

───────────────── ★ ─────────────────

CHAPTER FIVE

POLITICS:
PUP TENT REPUBLICANISM

As far as Simon Rosenberg is concerned, the 42 million Latinos who live in the United States have already shown that they have the political clout to turn a national election. It happened in 2000, he explained in an interview. It all came down to Florida. Al Gore was outspent in the Hispanic community by Bush, ten-to-one. The issue of whether or not Hispanics can determine who is president of the United States is settled.

A Democratic strategist, Rosenberg is a veteran of Bill Clinton's first presidential campaign. Today he runs the New Democratic Network, a center-left think tank based in Washington, D.C. Rosenberg is not one of those Beltway denizens so driven by partisanship as to be incapable of giving any credit to the other side. He tells me he spent the first six years of the Bush presidency admiring the "extraordinarily sophisticated and competent" efforts of Republican strategists—namely, Karl Rove, Matthew Dowd, and Ken Mehlman—to win over Latino voters.

In the past twenty years there's been a vast increase in the number of foreign-born, Spanish-dominant voters in the United States, says Rosenberg. About 8 percent of the national electorate is now Hispanic, and it's growing fast. Moreover, some 50 percent of the Hispanic electorate are foreign-born individuals who grew up speaking Spanish. That's an increase from just 20 percent in 1988, and most of Bush's gains among Latinos were from this group.

What this means, says Rosenberg, is that in essence, you have to become bilingual and bicultural to be competitive as a majority party in the twenty-first century. And the Republicans figured that out before the Democrats did. Latinos are projected to become 20 percent of the electorate by 2020 and one-quarter of the population by 2050. Bush realized that being on the wrong side of this demographic wave is the kind of thing that can relegate a party to minority status for a long time.

Even in 2004, says Rosenberg, the Democrats still hadn't really grasped what was happening. "[John] Kerry ran no significant campaign in Spanish. They were barely present in the southwestern states. They were taking the

Hispanic vote for granted. They thought it was a base vote. But obviously it became one of the most viable swing votes in American politics." Another top strategist, Joe Lockhart, who advised the Kerry campaign, agrees that Democrats were caught off-guard in 2004, telling *The New York Times*, "It was an election where they [the Republicans] knew more than we did."

Perhaps the Democrats finally have gotten their act together with respect to the importance of this vote. The 2008 Democratic Convention will be held in Colorado, where Latinos are by far the fastest-growing ethnic group and now number 19 percent of the population. The Democratic National Committee chose Nevada, another state with a large and growing Hispanic population, to vote second in the 2008 presidential primary calendar. New Mexico governor Bill Richardson and Connecticut senator Chris Dodd, two bilingual long shots for the Democratic nomination, nevertheless entered the race and speak Spanish everywhere they go.

But as Democrats attempt to make up ground in 2008 with this newly identified Latino cohort, the best thing they may have going for them is a bad stumble by the GOP in 2006. That was the year Republicans tried to turn Latino immigration into a midterm election wedge issue, like abortion or gay marriage. Not only did the strategy fail—Republicans lost their majority in the House and the Senate—but the party may have gone some distance toward undoing Bush's large gains among a swelling and increasingly important voting bloc.

"I thought the Republicans had probably passed the tipping point on this thing with Latinos," says Rosenberg. "I thought the Democrats had been caught flat-footed, that Bush and Dowd had moved an unbelievably powerful strategic chess piece. Then the Republicans decided to hold those field hearings. I said, 'I can't believe they're really going to do this.'"

"Those field hearings" were the brainchild of Dennis Hastert, Roy Blunt, James Sensenbrenner, and other Republican leaders in the House of Representatives, who in the spring of 2006 were desperate for a GOP campaign issue as the November elections approached. The situation in Iraq was worsening, as reflected in the president's low approval ratings. Social Security reform had gotten no traction. House Majority Leader Tom DeLay was mired in a high-profile scandal that would ultimately run him out of office. And economic conservatives at outfits like The Heritage Foundation, the Cato Institute, *National Review*, and *The Wall Street Journal* editorial page were dogging congressional Republicans about their fiscal incontinence. As Club for Growth chairman Pat Toomey wrote, presciently, in the *New York Post* that summer, "Like a drug addict who focuses all his energy on scoring his next fix with no regard for the long-term consequences, the GOP majority in Congress is on a spending bender that may ultimately lead it to hit rock bottom as the minority party."

The GOP wanted desperately to change the subject, and they decided that the illegal alien "crisis" was just the ticket. In fact, there was no crisis, other than the one manufactured by opponents of immigration. Illegal entries peaked in 2000, under President Clinton, and are down by a third since then. But the Republican leadership wasn't about to let such minor details stand in the way of playing up an issue that is perennially ripe for demagoguery. Earlier in the spring the Senate had passed an immigration bill along the lines of what the White House wanted. The legislation included more enforcement measures but also a guest-worker program with an eye to the future labor needs of the U.S. economy. In addition, the Senate bill allowed the estimated 12 million illegal aliens in the United States to earn legal status if they met certain requirements.

But rather than conferencing with the Senate to hash out a compromise, the House decided to spend the spring and summer of 2006 sabotaging the bill by denouncing it as "amnesty." Republicans held a series of town hall–type meetings around the country. In theory, the purpose was to discuss immigration reform. In practice, however, the purpose of the hearings was to rally the conservative base. GOP congressmen, particularly those in closely contested races, would use immigration to distance themselves from an unpopular president.

In other words, Republicans didn't want to solve a problem so much as exploit an issue in hopes of turning out the despondent GOP faithful. Republicans believed, with reason, that heavy turnout facilitated GOP gains in 2002 and 2004, and they were terrified that their base would stay home in November. Politicians are famous for their inability to see past the next election, and congressional Republicans in 2006 were no different. They covered their ears to warnings from Bush, Mehlman, and Rove that the strategy could backfire and spent the months leading up to the midterms desperately trying to demonize illegal aliens. Up to this point, Mexican immigration was such a nonissue in American politics that it never even came up in the 2004 presidential debates. But by November 2006, Republicans and their conservative allies in talk radio and cable news would turn it into a raucous national theme.

The GOP spent tens of millions of dollars on television ads that portrayed Latino immigrants as dangerous criminals and in some cases even compared them to Islamic terrorists. The spots didn't only run in border states, either. They could be seen in places like Pennsylvania, where the Latino population is relatively small and consists mainly of Puerto Ricans, who are U.S. citizens. One Republican ad, which suggested that supporters of the president's approach to immigration reform were soft on terrorism, ran in southwestern Ohio, where the only people crossing the border are from . . . Kentucky.

Restrictionist Losers

The strategy bombed, of course, even in places where illegal immigration is a huge problem and even among Republican candidates defined by their opposition to it. In Arizona, which is ground zero in the border wars, Representative J. D. Hayworth and Randy Graf were trounced. "Hayworth, who is so proud of his desire to turn the U.S. into a single gated community that he wrote a book about it, lost handily," wrote *The Wall Street Journal* in an editorial that appeared just after the election. "So did Randy Graf, another anti-immigration absolutist who ran for an open seat in a district that borders Mexico and sees more illegal immigrant traffic than perhaps any other congressional seat in the nation."

Moreover, as the editorial went on to explain, these Democratic gains in Arizona came in solid Republican congressional districts that Bush won easily two years earlier. Graf was attempting to succeed Republican Representative Jim Kolbe, an eleven-term incumbent who was retiring. Kolbe, who favored Bush's approach to immigration, had won re-election in 2004 with 60 percent of the vote. Graf lost 54 percent to 42 percent, after having won a GOP primary against a candidate with views similar to Kolbe's who could have kept the seat Republican.

Elsewhere in the country, Republican candidates who focused on immigration also fared poorly. In Indiana, Representative John Hostettler, another outspoken restrictionist, won just 39 percent of the vote in his losing bid for a seventh term. Hostettler's district was so Republican that John Kerry won only 38 percent of the vote there in 2004. In Colorado, Representative Bob Beauprez made opposition to illegal aliens the centerpiece of his run for governor. His Democratic opponent bested him by 15 percentage points. What's more, the Republican candidate who ran to replace Beauprez in the House, and appropriated much of his restrictionist rhetoric, also lost by nearly as much.

GOP Senate candidates like Tom Kean, Jr. in New Jersey and Mike McGavick in Washington State, who took increasingly hard line stances on immigration as Election Day approached, still lost to vulnerable Democratic incumbents. Pennsylvania's Rick Santorum, who ranked number four in the GOP Senate leadership, spent the summer of 2006 trying to convince voters that Mexican immigrants were a national security threat. He lost 59 percent to 41 percent.

It's possible, even probable, that the situation in Iraq sealed the fate of Republicans in the midterm elections, and that GOP immigrant-bashing didn't play a major role in the "thumping" the party took, to use President Bush's term. But there's also strong evidence that perceived GOP nativism did significant damage to the party's Latino outreach efforts. Which means that immigration restrictionism not only couldn't help Republicans hang on to Congress but also might have made it more difficult for them to win state and national elections going forward.

There's also this irony to mull: In 2005 and 2006, the

Bush administration had been making a concerted effort to reach out to black voters, even though Bush had done poorly among them in both 2000 and 2004. In July of 2006, Bush addressed the NAACP's annual convention and spoke frankly about the party's history with blacks. In 2005 and 2006 alone, Ken Mehlman spoke to more than fifty black audiences nationwide, including the NAACP and the National Urban League, acknowledging that Republicans in the past had tried "to benefit politically from racial polarization" and that "we were wrong." So at the same time that Bush and Mehlman were looking to bury the so-called southern strategy with respect to blacks, House Republicans were looking to employ it with respect to Hispanics.

And they may have succeeded, even if the tactic itself failed to produce the intended result. The Republican share of the Latino vote grew from 21 percent in 1996, to 35 percent in 2000, to 44 percent in 2004, according to exit polls. But in 2006, just 29 percent of Latinos told exit pollsters that they voted Republican. A June 2007 poll showed that Hispanics now identify themselves as Democrats rather than Republicans by 51 percent to 21 percent, a remarkable turnaround for a party that had doubled its share of the Latino vote inside of a decade. The question now is whether Republicans can patch things up with Hispanics in time for the 2008 presidential election. But the mystery is why so many conservatives behave as if it doesn't matter.

Bush clearly thinks it's unwise to alienate this growing group of voters, partly because he personally believes in racial and ethnic outreach and partly because he wants to avoid the Californianization of the Republican Party. In 1990, four years before Bush was elected governor of Texas, Pete Wilson, another Republican with presidential ambitions, was elected governor of California. In his first year in office, Wilson signed off on a huge tax increase to help close a budget gap. It didn't work. The tax hike produced less than half of the revenue that had been projected. And having upset his conservative base and damaged his approval rating, Wilson needed to change the subject as he began running for a second term.

And so he did. Wilson started harping on illegal immigration as the source of the state's fiscal woes. And he threw his support behind Proposition 187, a referendum that denied illegal immigrants and their children access to education and health care and required public employees to report illegals to immigration authorities. Wilson ran ads that showed people scurrying across the freeway while a voice-over boomed, "They just keep coming!" Proposition 187 passed easily, Wilson was reelected, and Republican restrictionists today point to the episode as proof that anti-immigration can work successfully as a wedge issue.

But the Wilson experience lends itself to other interpretations as well, and one is that opposition to immigration can lead to shallow, fleeting victories that cause deep, long-term political damage. The real story of Proposition 187, which ultimately was gutted by the courts, is the decline of GOP strength in California. Wilson won re-election in 1994, but he also managed to drive Latino voters into the arms of Democrats. Not only did his support in the Hispanic electorate fall from 47 percent in 1990 to 25 percent in 1994, but the ethnic voting patterns ran against the GOP for another decade. For three successive elections Republicans lost state assembly seats, a number of which were in districts where Hispanics were the critical voting bloc. Galvanized Latinos also registered to vote en masse—spiking their numbers from about 10 percent of the electorate in 1994 to about 15 percent in 1998—and many more were pulling the lever for Dems.

Wilson's perceived animosity toward Latinos even spilled over into other nonwhite voting blocs. For example, there was a drop in GOP support among Chinese and Korean voters, many of whom are small business owners in the state and who have a history of voting Republican. Given that Asians have surpassed blacks and are now the third-largest racial/ethnic voting bloc in California (after Latinos and whites) such secondary damage is not insignificant.

Wilson's would-be Republican successor, Dan Lungren, managed just 17 percent of the Latino vote in 1998 and was trounced by Gray Davis, who was supported by a whopping 78 percent of Latino voters. These days, Republican U.S. Senate candidates regularly lose there. The state has been blue in presidential contests for twenty years, and it took a unique politician like Arnold Schwarzenegger for the GOP to win back the governor's mansion in 2003. Oh, and you might have noticed that Woodrow remains the only Wilson to have occupied the Oval Office.

Meanwhile, down in Texas, another border state with a large share of illegal immigrants, George W. Bush took a different tack. Bush was the un-Wilson. He publicly denounced Prop 187, embraced newcomers, and earned the trust and support of Latinos, even increasing his share of the Hispanic vote when he was re-elected in 1998. In lieu of Wilson-style us-versus-them rhetoric, Bush labored to define the GOP as an inclusive, progrowth, forward-looking party. And most significantly, Bush rode his big-tent strategy all the way to the White House, while Wilson rode his into the dustbin of history and left behind a deep hole for Golden State Republicans to dig themselves out of.

LATINO SWINGERS

Michael Sokolove, writing in *The New York Times*, once noted that "the electoral math for Democrats begins with an assumption of capturing something like 90 percent of the African-American vote." And they usually come pretty close. Some 85 percent of blacks self-identify as Democrats, while fewer than 10 percent align with Republicans. Bill Clinton won more than 80 percent of the black vote in 1992 and 1996. Al Gore won 90 percent in 2000, and John Kerry won 88 percent in 2004. Black fealty to the political left is such that Democrats don't really have to battle the GOP for the black vote, so much as they have to battle apathy. Today's black electorate has made it clear that they will vote Democrat or stay home.

The left has no such claims on today's Latino vote, as even the more partisan Democrats acknowledge. "The great majority of Hispanics arrived in America in this half century and they are clearly in the process of forming party attachments," writes Stanley Greenberg, a Democratic pollster and advisor to Clinton and Gore. Greenberg found that Latinos are four times as likely as Anglos to give a "don't know" answer when asked which party they support, and that Mexicans in particular "are as likely as Anglos to say they are independents (33 percent) and to shift marginally their party allegiance toward Republicans with rising income and education."

Despite this political reality, however, many Republicans are happy to concede the Latino vote to Democrats rather than work for it. They continue to behave as if black and Latino voters are joined at the hip. Not only does the attitude that Hispanics are lost to the GOP betray a shocking lack of confidence in the appeal of Republicanism, but it also betrays an ignorance of U.S. political history.

"Starting with the civil rights movement, and with racial preferences and quotas being extended to Latinos, there was an assumption on the part of liberals that they were just like blacks," said Michael Barone in an interview. "But there are lots of differences." Barone, a political historian, said that the black political experience in the United States more closely resembles the Irish, while Latinos seem to be following the route taken by Italian immigrants.

Blacks in the rural South headed north in the great migration that began during World War II. Like the Irish immigrants who came a century earlier, they were fleeing societies in which they were second-caste citizens. With some exceptions, both groups generally lacked much entrepreneurial experience. They had been slaves and sharecroppers, peasants and serfs, with no opportunity to become Homo economicus. They looked to government as a means to change their caste status. They tended to gravitate toward the kinds of public sector jobs that the Democrats specialized in creating.

"The Irish loved those government patronage jobs sought through politics and run hierarchically like the Roman Catholic Church, a comparison that Pat Moynihan makes in *Beyond the Melting Pot*," said Barone. "Blacks are a little different in that black churches are more entrepreneurial and less hierarchical, but you still have political leaders like [former Washington, D.C., mayor] Marion Barry putting 55,000 people on the payroll of a city with 550,000 people."

Italians and Latinos, by contrast, come from societies with low levels of trust in public institutions, according to Barone. You trust your family and you work hard. You don't attract attention. This mind-set doesn't automatically turn you into a Republican, but it does mean that the Dems don't have a lock on your vote. So while the Irish for many decades voted uniformly Democratic nearly everywhere in the country (like today's blacks), Italians voted differently in different places (like today's Latinos). In some places there were WASP-Italian Republican alliances against the Irish Democrats. In other places Italians became Democrats.

In 2004, Bush won more than 40 percent of the Hispanic vote in Texas, New Mexico, and Arizona. In New York, New Jersey, California, Nevada, and Illinois, he won less than 40 percent but more than 20 percent. In Florida, he won the Hispanic vote outright, with 56 percent. "Latinos vote more like their neighbors," said Barone. "In East L.A. they're voting 90 percent Democrat, but when you get down to Santa Ana, in Orange County, they're voting about 52 percent Democrat. And nationally, if you're looking at around 60–40 Democrat in the 2004 election, that's already closer to whites, who were at 58–42, than it is to blacks, who were something like 90–10." Clearly the Latino vote is not (yet) "lost" to Republicans today. And if that does eventually happen, it will result from a GOP self-fulfilling prophecy.

FOOL'S GOLD

As a voting issue, immigration restrictionism is political pyrite. It's often likened to economic protectionism because both tend to poll better than they perform on Election Day.

Americans may rail against illegal aliens in telephone surveys, but election results have shown time and again that it's seldom the issue that decides someone's vote. The lesson for the GOP is that hostility to immigrants is not a political winner. That's been the lesson in the past, and given demographic trends, as well as a voting public that is more racially and ethnically tolerant than at any time in U.S. history, it's likely to be the lesson in the future. Unfortunately, it's not a lesson that some conservatives are in danger of learning anytime soon.

In an interview in early 2007, President Bush told me he was concerned that internal Republican disagreement over immigration was sending the wrong message to voters. "I don't want our party to be viewed as anti-anybody," said Bush. "If you get labeled as anti-people, you can't win elections." When I asked what was driving the dispute, he first replied: "I think conservatives tend to want to enforce the law," and then added, "yet the system that has sprung up as a result of [current] law is inhumane in many ways." Elaborating, the president said: "People want to be here so badly to put food on the table for their families that they're willing to get into the bottoms of eighteen-wheelers, for example. There's a whole hotel industry providing safe houses on both sides of the border. There's an interior transportation industry. There's document forgery taking place. There's a whole infrastructure that has sprung up as a result of a system that's not working."

Aside from that, said Bush, "this is an emotional issue,"

and he worried that some conservatives had let their emotions get the better of them. "It's interesting," said Bush. "There have been periods in our history where nativism has had a strong appeal. Sometimes nativism, isolationism, and protectionism all run hand in hand. We got to be careful about that in the United States. The 1920s was a period of high tariff, high tax, no immigration. And the lesson of the 1920s ought to be a reminder of what is possible for future presidents."

In 2007, immigration restrictionism on the right, if anything, intensified, particularly on talk radio. Despite losing the House and Senate in the previous year, President Bush and Karl Rove thought passing immigration reform and broadening the GOP base might still be possible. A bipartisan Senate bill cosponsored in 2006 by Ted Kennedy and John McCain provided a viable framework for comprehensive reform that would include more border enforcement, a guest-worker program, and a path to citizenship for illegals already in the country.

The immigration polls varied widely based on how questions were phrased. But any survey that presented the option of allowing illegal workers to remain here—and earn legal status by meeting certain requirements—garnered an overwhelmingly positive response from Republicans, Democrats, and Independents alike. Typical was a June 2007 *Wall Street Journal*/NBC News poll, which reported that 75 percent of Republicans found it "not realistic" to require undocumented immigrants in the United States to return home to seek legal status, and 81 percent said it was unrealistic to seek their deportation.

SAY ANYTHING

With Bush still in office, and Democrats sympathetic to his position running Congress, there was a possibility of moving forward on the issue. But it didn't happen, in large part because Rush Limbaugh, Sean Hannity, and Laura Ingraham were having none of it. Nor were Hugh Hewitt, Dennis Prager, Mike Gallagher, Glenn Beck, Bill Bennett, Michael Savage, and other popular radio personalities with millions of listeners. Some of us watched in disbelief as principled conservatives morphed into reactionary populists. These profiles in courage used immigration to declare their independence from Bush at a time when he was highly unpopular. Gee, how brave.

Limbaugh and Bennett, who normally worship at the political altar of pro-immigrant Ronald Reagan, were instead urging Republicans to follow in the footsteps of Pete Wilson. Ingraham regularly denounced the Republican "elites" supporting comprehensive immigration reform at the supposed expense of America's working class. Ingraham, self-styled enemy of "elites," is a Connecticut-bred, Ivy League–educated, former Supreme Court law clerk. But on immigration, she sounded like Sally Field in *Norma Rae*.

And then there were the conservative talkers who took cues from Ann Coulter and simply relished in stoking racial and ethnic divisions. Beck described Mexican illegals as either "terrorists," or people who "can't make a living in their own dirtbag country." Michael Savage repeatedly called on listeners to "burn the Mexican flag" in opposition to immigrants. "Go out in the street and show you're a man, burn ten Mexican flags," he said. "Put one in a window upside down and tell them to go back where they came from."

Michael Medved, one of the few pro-immigrant conservatives on the air, told me, "The behavior of people on talk radio has been so despicable and so irresponsible that it really makes me question what passes for the conservative movement today." Medved said many of these conservative shock jocks don't really believe what they're saying and that some—like Limbaugh, Hannity, and Prager—had adopted a much more moderate tone on immigration in the past. While Medved personally rejects the populist allure of restrictionism, he certainly understands the temptation. "You can light up the phone lines instantly with immigrant-bashing," said Medved. "You get callers right away." Medved's worried, however, that there will be a political price to pay on the right at some point in the future. "It's a very, very sick underbelly of American conservatism, and unless we confront it and make it clear that it has no place in the Republican Party, we are going to go the way of the Know-Nothings."

Fred Barnes, a veteran conservative journalist at FOX

News and *The Weekly Standard*, also credits the talk radio drum beat with helping to kill immigration reform last year. "The ability of talk radio to produce noise on the right when they agree is remarkable," said Barnes. "They can generate mail. They can generate phone calls." Barnes, too, thinks there will be repercussions. "The defeat [of the Senate bill] will have lasting damage for the simple reason that Hispanics were paying attention to it. For some reason opponents of immigration don't think they are. But my impression is that immigrants say, 'We're either welcome or we're not.' And the average person doesn't distinguish between Bush and the party."

The base was feeling blue, and with immigration talk radio hosts found an issue where the public agreed with them. "But sometimes political issues get out of hand emotionally, and this one did," says Barnes. "You couldn't reason with these people. Conservatives got themselves into a position where you couldn't talk to them. Take someone like Laura Ingraham, who I know and like. After Bush gave his speech [saying that immigration restrictionists] were not for what's best for America, she started saying he's questioning our patriotism. 'Questioning our patriotism' is what Ted Kennedy and John Kerry say whenever you disagree with them on defense or foreign policy. I thought that argument was totally the preserve of liberals, but I guess not."

Conservative critics of the Senate bill worried that the interior enforcement provisions, which called for cracking down on employers who hire illegals, would never be enforced, and that the rest amounted to rewarding people who'd broken the law by entering the country illegally. Anything short of requiring 12 million illegal immigrants, regardless of whether they'd been in the country twenty months or twenty years, to leave was denounced loudly and repeatedly as "amnesty." And once amnesty entered the discussion, the discussion was over, as far as the restrictionists were concerned. They argued that we already tried amnesty, with the Immigration Control and Reform Act of 1986 (ICRA), and it didn't reduce illegal border crossings. In fact, they said, it encouraged them, and now we have at least four times as many illegals as we did twenty years ago.

Ed Meese, a former attorney general under President Reagan and a critic of the Senate bill, laid this out in a *New York Times* op-ed, where he wrote, "Like the amnesty bill of 1986, the current Senate proposal would place those who have resided illegally in the United States on a path to citizenship, provided they meet a similar set of conditions and pay a fine and back taxes." Like so many other opponents of the bill, Meese didn't say what, exactly, should be done with the 12 million illegals already here, given that the public has shown no appetite for deporting them. He just wanted to reiterate that "the 1986 act did not solve our illegal immigration problem" and dismiss the 2007 Senate bill as, by and large, a replica of what Congress passed two decades earlier.

Meese mentioned in passing that there was "widespread document fraud" and "a failure of political will" to crackdown on businesses under ICRA. In fact the decision to deputize business owners as immigration agents was disastrous. In his discussion of the 1986 law in *A Nation by Design*, Aristide Zolberg says that the strategy was "doomed from the start." Employer sanctions had been touted politically since the 1950s as an effective deterrent to illegal immigration, but few labor economists thought they'd actually work. Why? Supply and demand. "[T]he flow across the border was largely shaped by economic conditions on both sides," writes Zolberg, "and these powerful 'push' and 'pull' factors outweighed the costs that sanctions imposed on either employers or employees."

But in addition to being at odds with Economics 101, the 1986 law added mounds of red tape to the process of starting and running a company in the United States—the type of protectionist hurdles that the left normally champions. The new regulations "entailed a wholesale transformation of American business practices, requiring each of the country's 7 million employers to maintain on file for three years new forms attesting that they had checked the work eligibility and identification documents of every employee," writes Zolberg. "On the government side, enforcement entailed a monumental and unprecedented joint undertaking by the Department of Labor and the Department of Justice, for which they lacked organizational capacity, and failed to obtain adequate funding, in keeping with the White House's thorough lack of sympathy for any expansion of the regulatory apparatus."

That would be the Reagan White House, by the way. When Meese and other restrictionist conservatives lament the "lack of political will" under Reagan to increase regulations and raid businesses for hiring willing workers, free-market proponents say, "Good for the Gipper." Yes, Reagan signed a bill that included employer sanctions. He operated at the nexus of ideas and politics, and he had to make some accommodation for what was achievable. He was a practical politician and that was the price of passing reform. But Reagan, whose views on immigration ran to John Winthrop, not Madison Grant, was never a big fan of the "interior enforcement" provisions, and it showed in his lack of enthusiasm for sanctioning businesses.

Unlike the restrictionists today who claim to speak in his name, Reagan understood the economic upshot of free and flexible labor markets. As a Californian, he understood the role of immigrant labor in agribusiness and other industries. And as a small-government conservative, he understood the unfairness and illogic of punishing companies for failing to detect and oust illegal aliens in their midst, especially when immigration authorities had themselves proven so inept at performing the same task.

George W. Bush understands this, too, and has argued that our immigration policies should be brought into compliance with the needs of our economy. But his opponents on the political right want the status quo. They want the current laws enforced and never mind the difficulty, impracticality, and potential economic damage. These folks essentially denounced the Reagan administration for not unleashing armies of G-men to harass business owners and immigrants who are freely contracting for labor. And they were terrified that if the Senate bill passed, Bush might be too much like Reagan in this regard. Oh, the horror!

AMNESTY AIN'T THE ANSWER

It may well be factually correct to say, as comprehensive reform critics like Meese have, that the amnesty provisions of the 1986 act didn't solve the illegal alien problem. But it's also highly misleading. After all, ICRA's border enforcement provisions—and the numerous subsequent enhancements—haven't stanched the illegal flow, either, but that hasn't stopped Tom Tancredo from calling for still more security measures to be put in place.

The reality is that the amnesty provisions in ICRA weren't destined to bring us any closer to stopping illegal immigration than were employer sanctions. Illegal immigration to the United States is a function, first and foremost, of too many foreigners chasing too few visas. Some 400,000 people enter the country illegally each year—a direct consequence of the fact that our current policy is to make available just five thousand visas annually for low-skilled workers. If we want to reduce the number of illegal entries, the most sensible course is to provide more legal ways for people to come.

This could be done through some sort of guest-worker program or by lifting the quota on green cards or both. The means matter less than the end, which should be to give U.S. businesses legal access to foreign workers going forward. ICRA did not do that, which is why it didn't solve the problem. The 3 million illegal aliens who were brought into status in 1986 had already been absorbed by the U.S. labor market. The problem with ICRA is that its designers ignored the *future* labor needs of U.S. employers. After the amnesty took effect, our economy continued to grow and hungered for more foreign workers. But since the legal channels available were not sufficiently expanded, migrants once again began coming illegally, which is how today's illegal population grew to its current size. Another amnesty, by itself, will do no more to "solve" this problem in the long run than the first one did.

It's unfortunate that the "no amnesty" crowd was able to suck up so much oxygen in this debate. Talk radio hosts, cable news anchors, and former attorneys general used the term, quite effectively, to end conversations. And restrictionists in Congress invoked it as a political slogan to kill any reform. But from a public policy perspective, the fate of the 12 million illegals already here is largely a side issue, a problem that will take care of itself in time if we get the other reforms right.

As was the case in 1986, the United States today has easily absorbed the current illegal workforce, as evidenced by our steady economic growth and low unemployment rate in recent years. These foreigners are helping to expand our economy by filling (and creating) jobs, not pinching them from natives. They're working hard, starting businesses, marrying, having children, and assimilating. If their presence here is a problem, then it is a self-correcting one. In time, they will grow old and pass on with the rest of us. Policy makers would do better to focus less on whether to amnesty or deport them and more on how to stop feeding their numbers going forward. And history, in addition to economics, suggests that the best way to do that is by providing more legal ways for foreign workers to come.

We know from past experience that Mexican migrants coming here to feed their families will use the front door if it's available to them. Crazy as it sounds, they prefer to live here legally rather than in the shadows, enriching human smugglers and document forgers. Nearly seven decades ago, the United States faced labor shortages in agriculture stemming from World War II, and growers turned to the Roosevelt administration for help. The result was the Bracero Program, which allowed hundreds of thousands of Mexican farm workers to enter the country legally as seasonal laborers. In place from 1942 to 1964, the program was jointly operated by the Departments of State, Labor, and Justice, and administered by the Immigration and Naturalization Service. And it provides strong evidence that the economic law of supply and demand doesn't stop at the Rio Grande.

Stuart Anderson, a former INS official who has studied the Bracero period, found a direct trade-off between the number of visas made available and the number of illegal entries, which the government measures by tallying border apprehensions. As the program was expanded in the post-WWII years to meet the labor needs of a booming U.S. economy, illegal border crossings fell off a cliff. Between 1953 and 1959, they dropped by some 95 percent. A 1980 Congressional Research Service report concluded that, "without question," the Bracero Program was "instrumental in ending the illegal alien problem of the mid-1940s and 1950s."

Beginning in 1960, the program was phased out after opposition from unions. And since nothing comparable emerged to replace it, illegal entries began to rise again. The point isn't that we need to resurrect the Bracero Program, or that a guest-worker program alone will stop illegal immigration from Mexico. But there's no reason we can't put a Bracero-like program in place with the proper worker protections and get a similar result. The program worked because it acknowledged human nature and economic reality. Current policy, with its lopsided emphasis on enforcement, ignores both. The problem with the 1986 act is not that it included an amnesty provision but that it didn't include something along the lines of a Bracero Program. George W. Bush and the comprehensive reformers didn't want to make the same mistake.

---★---

CHAPTER SIX

HOMELAND SECURITY: FORTRESS AMERICA?

In the summer of 2006, *Reason* magazine, the libertarian monthly, devoted an issue to America's immigrant past. Restrictionists tend to have selective memories, and the essays inside provided historical context for the various political, economic, and social arguments informing the current debate. But what really recommends the issue are the half-dozen vintage late-nineteenth- and early-twentieth-century illustrations that accompany the text. The images, culled from long-forgotten periodicals like *Judge* and *The Wasp*, are vivid reminders of the unoriginality of today's immigrant bashers.

One drawing, from 1901 depicts the United States as a

giant magnet attracting "Oriental diseases," "Dago criminals," and other people with distinct simian features who
are labeled simply "filth" or "dirt." The caption beneath
reads: "The only bad feature of our prosperity."

A 1903 *Judge* print, "The High Tide of Immigration—
a National Menace," depicts immigrants as riffraff washing ashore, where Uncle Sam stands clinging to a boulder
that reads, "Danger to American Ideas and Institutions."
Beneath the drawing is a caption reminiscent of the non
sequiturs favored by Lou Dobbs and Pat Buchanan: "Immigration statistics for the past year show that the influx
of foreigners was the greatest in our history," it reads, "and
also that the hard-working . . . [Americans] are now being
supplanted by the criminals and outlaws of all Europe." In
other words, today's fear that America is accepting too
many immigrants (and the wrong kinds, besides) is the
same old, same old. Nor are the methods used to stir up
anti-immigrant passions in the twenty-first century much
different from those of yore, when populist elites also at-
tempted to scare natives into believing that new arrivals
threaten not only our economic prosperity but also our
safety.

And like today's nativists, yesteryear's weren't averse to
fudging the facts to further an anti-immigrant agenda. Another 1903 *Judge* illustration, "The Unrestricted Dumping-
Ground," likens immigrants to rats scurrying into the
United States "direct from the slums of Europe daily." The
vermin have human heads with swarthy complexions and

wear hats or bandannas that read "Mafia," "Anarchist," and "Socialist." One holds a knife with a blade that reads "Assassination"; another carries a pistol with "Murder" written on the grip. In the upper-left-hand corner of the drawing is a likeness of President William McKinley, who had been fatally shot two years earlier by Leon Czolgosz, an anarchist, at the Pan-American Exhibition in Buffalo, New York. Czolgosz was not an immigrant but a U.S. native, born in Detroit. His *parents* had immigrated from Poland. Minor detail.

CRIMINAL ALIEN NATION?

These days, opponents of immigration aren't much interested in details and accuracy either, preferring, as demagogues do, half-truths and innuendo. Whether discussing everyday crime or homeland security, the objective is to play to people's fears and prejudices. Tom Tancredo declares that "there are 9 to 11 million illegal aliens living amongst us right now who have never had a criminal background check and have never been screened through any terrorism databases." And Pat Buchanan adds, "The enemy is already inside the gates. How many others among our 11 million 'undocumented' immigrants are ready to carry out truck bombings, assassinations, sabotage, skyjackings?" Everything from drunk driving to murder receives extra attention when an undocumented immigrant is involved, leaving the impression, however unsupported by the facts, that the country is in the throes of an illegal alien crime wave.

On July 23, 2007, two men entered a home in Cheshire, Connecticut, and held a husband, wife, and their two daughters—ages seventeen and eleven—hostage for seven hours. The husband was beaten unconscious with a baseball bat, then bound and left in the basement for dead. The wife and daughters were raped, strangled, tied to their beds, doused with gasoline, and set on fire. Only the husband, who awoke to his wife's screams and, still bound, crawled out of the house in search of help, survived. The two suspects, Joshua Komisarjevsky and Steven Hayes, were lifelong criminals out on parole. Komisarjevsky had twenty-one prior felony convictions; Hayes had seventeen. They were caught by police while fleeing the scene.

Less than two weeks later, on August 4, three Newark, New Jersey, college students—two twenty-year-olds and an eighteen-year-old—were lined up against a wall, forced to kneel, and fatally shot. A fourth shooting victim, age nineteen, was wounded but survived. As was the case in the Cheshire murders, the Newark victims had no criminal records. Also like the Connecticut case, the lead suspect in the New Jersey deaths, José Carranza, had repeated run-ins with the law. He'd been arrested three times before on felony charges, including child rape, but released on bail.

You might think these two triple homicides would prompt a national discussion about parole, bail, recidivism, and how a criminal justice system can defend keeping violent predators on such a long leash. In fact, the Cheshire murders received little attention from pundits outside of the Connecticut area. And no one much cared about the Newark incident either, until it was later revealed that Carranza was an illegal alien from Peru, at which point talk radio and cable news outlets nationwide could talk of little else. Immigrant foes presented Carranza as a typical Latino illegal alien, and his status dominated the discussion. What could have been a conversation about the inadequacies of our criminal justice system instead turned into a prolonged session of immigrant bashing.

Bill O'Reilly, who checks the immigration status of drunk drivers before deciding whether to discuss them on the air, said Newark had brought this tragedy on itself because the city had not deputized its police officers as immigration agents. Never mind that Newark's mayor, Cory Booker, campaigned for office on crime prevention. He is one of the sharpest urban leaders in the country, part of a small band of young black politicians who aren't afraid to challenge liberal orthodoxy on everything from taxes to school reform to crime. To O'Reilly, however, Booker was no better than his corrupt predecessor, Sharpe James. The commentator said Booker lacked "the will to protect people from crime and terrorism," and that "his city continues to allow criminal illegal aliens to commit crimes."

Others piled on. Referencing Carranza, Newt Gingrich said the "war here at home" against illegal aliens is "even more deadly than the war in Iraq and Afghanistan." Tom Tancredo even paid a visit to Newark to exploit the tragedy. He, too, fingered Booker and other officials as complicit in the murders because they had declared Newark a "sanctuary city" for illegals. "Their actions have directly contributed to the deaths of three promising young American kids," said Tancredo, standing on the steps of city hall.

So-called sanctuary policies adopted by dozens of major cities, including Los Angeles and New York, discourage municipal workers from assessing the immigration status of people using city services and then passing it on to federal immigration authorities. But in Newark, as elsewhere, the police are exempted from the sanctuary provisions during criminal investigations. That minor detail was omitted by O'Reilly, Gingrich, Tancredo, and others as they rushed to milk the situation for a few divisive sound bites. So was the fact that many big-city police departments don't want to be responsible for enforcing federal immigration laws because they say it makes them less effective at their day jobs. How so? People in immigrant communities who view the local police as deportation agents are less likely to report crimes and assist in investigations, which tends to make a city less safe.

WHO'S DRIVING U.S. CRIME RATES?

But using Carranza as a poster child for illegal immigration isn't merely opportunistic. It's also a gross distortion of reality, albeit a common one. One poll found that nearly 75 percent of Americans perceive a causal link between increased immigration and increased crime, which is even higher than the 60 percent who mistakenly believe that immigrants displace American workers. Certainly, Hollywood abets the misperception with popular fare like *The Godfather*, *Scarface*, and *The Sopranos*. Media reports on Colombian cocaine cartels and Salvadoran gangs also might lead people to believe that immigrants are responsible for higher crime rates. And then there's the fact that so many of today's newcomers share the demographic characteristics of native-born criminals: male Latinos with low-average levels of education and low-average wages. The assumption, which is shared by many politicians and public policy makers, is that the immigrants who fit this profile must be adversely affecting crime rates. Even immigrant-friendly George W. Bush has stated that "illegal immigration . . . brings crime to our communities."

Small wonder, then, that Congress's failure to overhaul immigration laws has led states to enact their own policies. In the first six months of 2007, more than 1,400 measures were considered by state legislatures nationwide, and 170 of them passed. In all, forty-one states adopted immigration laws last year. Some restricted illegal immigrants' access to housing or the labor market; others denied them education, health care, and driver's licenses. The goal, essentially, is to make life in the United States unbearable for illegals in the hope that they will voluntarily return to their homeland. Many Americans don't realize the difficulty, if not futility, of trying to make life in Ohio or Illinois more unbearable than life in some impoverished rural Mexican state like Jalisco or Zacatecas. They also don't realize that immigrants, regardless of their legal status, aren't driving crime in this country.

In 2005, the Federal Reserve Bank of Chicago published a study on immigrant incarceration rates. The authors, Kristin Butcher and Anne Morrison Piehl, found that "despite the widespread perception of a link between immigration and crime, immigrants have much lower institutionalization (incarceration) rates than the native born." They also reported that more recently arrived immigrants have the lowest comparative incarceration rates, "and that their relative rates of institutionalization have fallen over the last three decades." In 1980 the incarceration rate of foreign nationals was about one percentage point below natives; in 1990, it was a little more than one percentage point lower; and in 2000, it was almost three percentage points lower. Which means that talk of an immigrant "crime wave" was unsubstantiated by the facts thirty years ago, and it's even less true today.

These findings are even more remarkable (and at odds with common perceptions) when you consider that immigration, both legal and illegal, has ballooned in recent decades, a point made by Rubén Rumbaut and Walter Ewing in a 2007 study of immigrant criminality for the Immigration Policy Center (IPC). "Even as the undocumented population has doubled to 12 million since 1994, the violent crime rate in the United States has declined by 34.2 percent and the property crime rate has fallen 26.4 percent," write the authors. "Cities with large immigrant populations such as Los Angeles, New York, Chicago, and Miami also have experienced declining crime rates during this period."

Nor is this a matter of law-abiding immigrant professionals from places like China, South Korea, India, and Taiwan compensating for a criminally inclined Latino immigrant underclass. Data from the census, the Justice Department, and other sources show that "for every ethnic group without exception, incarceration rates among young men are lowest for immigrants, even those who are the least educated," write Rumbaut and Ewing. "This holds true especially for the Mexicans, Salvadorans, and Guatemalans who make up the bulk of the undocumented population."

Males between eighteen and thirty-nine who haven't completed high school comprise a majority of the U.S. prison population. They also represent a fair share of today's Latino immigrants. Still, the IPC study found that the incarceration rate among natives in 2000 was five times higher than that of the foreign-born, 3.5 percent versus 0.7 percent. Native-born Latino men were almost seven times more likely to be incarcerated than Latino immigrants. Even white Anglos are imprisoned at higher rates than foreign-born white men.

Anti-immigrant activists point to a 2005 Government Accountability Office (GAO) report and other studies estimating that around one-quarter of all federal prisoners in the United States are "criminal aliens." What these activists omit is the size of the federal prison system. According to the Department of Justice, approximately 8 percent of the 2.2 million people behind bars in the United States at the end of 2005 were in federal prisons. The majority of inmates are in state prisons (57 percent) or local jails (34 percent). In other words, the GAO report estimates that immigrants comprise 25 percent of a prison system that holds 8 percent of the country's inmates. It's also important to note that the high proportion of noncitizens in federal prisons is linked to the fact that immigration violations are federal offenses.

Still, the bottom line remains that noncitizens comprise a disproportionately small percentage of U.S. inmates overall. According to the Justice Department's latest figures, noncitizens are 7 percent of the U.S. population but only 6.4 percent of the prisoners.

"The problem of crime in the United States is not 'caused' or even aggravated by immigrants, regardless of their legal status," write Rumbaut and Ewing. "But the misperception that the opposite is true persists among policymakers, the media, and the general public, thereby undermining the development of reasoned public responses to both crime and immigration." The reality is that Americans have more reason to fear the native-born Joshua Komisarjevskys and Steven Hayeses than they do illegal aliens like Jose Carranza. Much more reason, in fact. We're not "importing crime." Our crime problems are homegrown, and it's hard to see how smearing immigrants will change that.

Conflating Latino Immigration and Terrorism

But what of the notion that immigrants from Latin America pose an undue terror threat? Conflating terrorism and illegal immigration has become popular in the wake of 9/11, though the logic isn't easy to follow. After all, we were attacked via jetliners by Islamists from the Middle East, all of whom entered the country legally. How would a wall across our southern border aimed at deterring Christian Latinos make us safer?

If anything, a fortification spanning our northern border with Canada would be in order. The U.S.–Canadian border is more than twice as long as its Mexican counterpart but has far fewer patrols. And Canada's asylum policies are much more forgiving than Mexico's, which has led to a far more extensive Muslim presence than can be found in Mexico. Muslim extremists in Canada have an infrastructure and logistics at the ready, which isn't the case in Mexico. Islamists could always make use of the vast smuggling networks in Latin America, one supposes, but that's something that's out of their control and exposes them to capture.

So far, no terrorist attack has been perpetrated by someone who sneaked into the United States through Mexico, let alone by a Mexican, Guatemalan, Salvadoran, Honduran, or any other foreign national from Latin America. That doesn't mean it can't or won't ever happen, but it does help explain why building fences and other barricades along the Rio Grande isn't at the top of the list for people who spend a lot of time thinking about homeland security.

"There are too many easier ways to get into the U.S., and the Mexican border isn't a particularly attractive one," says Jeremy Shapiro, a national security expert at the Brookings Institution. "The Mexican border is a very controlled border, relatively speaking. It's more patrolled than any of our other borders. That doesn't mean that a lot of people don't get in. It means that a relatively large number of people who try to get in get caught." In 2005, border patrol agents apprehended about 1.2 million foreigners, 90 percent of whom were Mexicans caught just inside the border. When you get caught, you're detained for a period and fingerprinted, the last thing you want if you're on a terrorist watch list. And if you're not in the system, well, then there's no reason to sneak in at all.

A drug dealer operating out of Central America may send a hundred mules north every month and expect, say, 75 percent to make it. But terrorist activities are too small to deal in those sorts of loss rates. Given the time and investment that goes into large-scale attacks, a 25 percent chance of getting caught is unacceptable. "It's not that you can't come through the Mexican border," says Shapiro. "It's just that it always makes more sense to come in through some other way. And a wall and 10,000 more border patrol agents isn't going to change that."

Obviously, homeland security for a nation our size requires prioritization. The United States has 216 airports and 143 seaports, where nearly 9 million containers are off-loaded every year. There are an additional 115 land facilities that serve as official ports of entry, handling car and truck traffic. The country has 500,000 bridges, 500 skyscrapers, nearly 200,000 miles of natural gas pipelines, and 2,900 power plants—more than 100 of which are nuclear. Then there are subways and shopping malls and countless other critical infrastructure, not to mention the human traffic. Some 30 million foreign nationals enter the United States annually, more than 95 percent of whom are tourists or business travelers. According to the Immigration and Customs Enforcement agency, in 2006 there were 750,000 foreign student and exchange visitors in the United States.

Given limited resources, protecting everything in equal proportion is not a viable option. Nor is putting an ankle bracelet on each visitor. Fortunately, however, every vulnerability is not a serious threat. It's possible that Al Qaeda is eyeing an edifice in suburban Santa Fe, but it's not plausible. Robert Leiken, a homeland security scholar at the Nixon Institute, noted that post-9/11, sealing the Mexican border has

"quite properly" not been a major focus of the Bush administration's antiterror strategy. "Latin America in general and
Mexico in particular are inhospitable to Muslim extremists in
ways Canada and our sea and air borders are not," says Leiken.
"There are at most a handful of Islamic terrorist cells in Latin
America, most notably Hezbollah smuggling and money laun-
dering operations in the lawless *Ciudad del Este* on the 'triple
frontier' where Argentina, Brazil, and Paraguay meet."

Michael O'Hanlon, another national security ace at
Brookings, thinks that as a general rule, it makes sense to
have not only secure borders but good databases on who
you're watching out for. And he supports, at a minimum, a
standardized, biometrically based national driver's license. But he adds, "The only thing dangerous here is
that the border itself is insecure, not that a lot of Latinos
are coming across it. I know of no evidence that there's
been a terrorist threat from a Latino virtually ever. There
are Latino criminals—the narco threat—but they aren't
terrorists."

SHRINKING THE HAYSTACK

Prior to 9/11, border security was divided among six Cabi-
net departments—State, Treasury, Justice, Transportation,
Agriculture, and Defense. The Department of Homeland
Security (DHS), established in 2002, brought together

twenty-two previously separate agencies within those departments. It now includes the Immigration and Customs Enforcement, Customs and Border Protection, and the Coast Guard. DHS has more than 200,000 employees, and its 2006 budget was $40 billion.

Reactionary populists of the Michelle Malkin variety want to do little more than throw additional resources at border patrol. Like liberals and failing public schools, they're convinced that more money is the answer. There's no place for sober cost-benefit analyses in the policy prescriptions of Malkin, Buchanan, Tancredo, and Dobbs, only indignation and ignorance. Like the Minutemen kooks she champions by name, Malkin wants illegal aliens detained at military bases, soldiers patrolling the Rio Grande, and a complete moratorium on visas for people from certain Muslim countries. She wants entering America to be "a fiercely guarded privilege." Literally.

But DHS officials say that the wiser course of action is a more comprehensive approach. Border barriers, human or otherwise, get you only so far. Only about half of the foreigners in the United States illegally evaded border controls. More than 40 percent entered legally but stayed too long or otherwise violated their visa. Just like the 9/11 terrorists. In other words, had the Army's Second Infantry Division been patrolling the border prior to 9/11, it still wouldn't have thwarted the attacks. Militarizing the border to stop the next Mohamed Atta is like taking a laxative to treat psoriasis.

We're better off reducing pressure on the border by giving economic migrants more legal ways to come. That would make it easier to weed out real security threats. The problem isn't a shortage of patrols so much as how existing patrols are being used. In an interview last year, I asked DHS Secretary Michael Chertoff about the Mexican border and homeland security. "The economic migrants are not a threat to national security," he said. "The problem they pose is that as long as we have to deal with them, they are decoys through which the threat can travel. As long as they support an illegal network of document fraud, they then create a marketplace that is also accessible to terrorists and criminals."

Chertoff likened illegal immigration from Mexico to "tall grass" that we need to "cut down to expose the people we're really worried about." It's "a distraction," he said, and it stretches our limited resources. "When you have a guy spending the day transporting, booking, processing, and deporting an economic migrant, he's not on the border watching for drug dealers and gang members," said Chertoff. "So both strategically and tactically, it's a drain on resources."

Tom Ridge, Chertoff's predecessor at DHS, struck a similar note. "Immigration itself and Mexican immigrants don't rank very high in terms of my concern about terrorism," he told me in an interview. "It's the [smuggling] network and 'other-than-Mexican' potential clients that can take advantage of that network" that he worried about. "It's not so much viewing the [Latino] immigrants themselves as security risks, because I don't think they are," said Ridge. "I've seen some of these young people that we've got detained at the detention centers and some of the ones that we've sent back. By and large, I think they just want to come here to work."

Neither Chertoff nor Ridge is averse to physical barriers along portions of the border, but both rejected the notion that we can simply wall off the terrorism threat. A more comprehensive approach is needed. Protecting the homeland, they insisted, requires deference to certain economic realities. "I don't think you can put up three thousand miles of fencing, but I think the five or six hundred miles that [Congress is considering] should be built," said Ridge. "But even if we maximize the defense approach as best we can, there will still be an economic incentive to get across the border. I don't see how you can have a good security policy without a good guest-worker program." As globalization continues, our relationship with Canada and Mexico will be even more important, he said. "And at the end of the day, both a defensive posture along the border and a means to legitimize those who seek to work here is . . . in our economic interests, our security interests, and our global interests."

Chertoff told me he was astonished by the arguments he heard coming from the political right during the 2007 debate over the Senate immigration bill, which would have created a path to legal status for illegal immigrants already in the country and a guest-worker program for future labor flows. "I've been surprised at how many conservatives don't really believe in the free market when it comes to immigration," he said. "And I'm only being partly facetious. First, some people just don't accept the figures. They don't accept that there's an expanding economy, that we've got low unemployment. They won't accept the fact that if you look at the demographics, my generation"—he was born in 1953—"is getting older. We will not want to be picking lettuce at age eighty and eighty-five. Everybody across the globe is facing this and we are, too, in terms of simply needing people to do certain work. Bringing in people to work ends up expanding the pie. They get money. They pay taxes. They buy goods and services."

Like Ridge, Chertoff said that any increased security measures aimed at stemming illegal immigration from Latin America should be paired with more lawful ways for migrants to enter the country and fill jobs. "The only way to truly get enforcement done is to create legal pathways to satisfy what is an undeniable work need," he said. Chertoff also favors giving the 12 million illegal aliens already here an opportunity to legalize their status, so that we know who's here and can regulate their activities. The objective is to reduce the size of the illegal alien haystack, so that officials can concentrate on real threats instead of chasing down Salvadorans here to hang drywall.

Chertoff had particular disdain for the so-called attrition approach to reducing illegal immigration. A favorite of enforcement-first conservative tub thumpers, the idea is that illegals will self-deport if we make things tough for them.

"Even assuming politically, and it's a counterfactual assumption, that you pass a bill that's entirely enforcement oriented," he said, "you still have the following dilemma":

> You have about 7 million people working [illegally] and the rest are their dependents. Many of them are rooted here. They may have their kids in school. And they've got jobs. If the employers fire these 7 million, who's going to do the work? I don't see that we have 7 million temporary workers teed up to come in right away. So it's not practical. The major cause of attrition, which would be drying up the employment, requires you to assume the employers will either put their businesses into bankruptcy or that you'll bring in 7 million replacements. Neither of those things is going to happen. Once you've disproved those two assumptions, why will there be attrition? Even if we could round up a thousand people a week, that would only be about fifty thousand a year. Do the math. How many years will it be? What are the odds of getting caught? And, remember, you've got a guy who's working and won't be fired. The chances that he's going to attrite himself out, so to speak, are negligible. I think the attrition argument is really benign neglect. And that's just amnesty, only it's amnesty without the visibility.

All nineteen of the 9/11 hijackers were Middle Eastern Arabs, just like more than 90 percent of the foreigners caught plotting or committing terrorist acts in the United States since the 1993 World Trade Center bombing. Given this pattern, extra scrutiny of immigrants and visitors from countries with links to terrorism is warranted. And after 9/11, the Justice Department began requiring visa holders from twenty mostly Arab and Muslim countries to register with immigration officials.

How interesting that those obsessed with illegal aliens from Mexico are so eager to link them with terrorism, while those tasked with homeland security consider economic migrants more of a distraction. As border patrol spokesman Xavier Rios put it to the Associated Press in 2007, "If there's a way that the pressure could be taken off the law enforcement piece of it by basically taking the economic migrant out of the mix, then we'll be well on our way to getting effective control of the border. . . . The majority of the folks that we apprehend are coming in for jobs."

Conflating illegal immigration and terrorism makes the country less safe, because the money and manpower spent keeping Mexican workers out of the country is not being spent keeping Middle Eastern terrorists at bay.

How We Got Here

Ridge and Chertoff also know the history of an enforcement-only approach to stopping illegal immigration from Mexico.

It's a history of misguided attempts to ignore the economic law of supply and demand. It's a history of underestimating the will of human beings to better their circumstances and provide for loved ones. It's a history of policy failure.

For most of the nineteenth century, the United States considered itself underpopulated. To guard against the perceived threat from Native Americans, we actively recruited immigrants from Europe and Asia, luring them with the promise of endless economic opportunity and religious freedom. U.S. employers paid for their voyage, and the federal government promised free land to immigrants willing to settle the frontier. Until the mid-1800s most of the Southwestern United States was still part of Mexico. In 1850, two years after the Treaty of Guadalupe Hidalgo officially ended the Mexican-American War, only about sixty thousand Mexicans lived in what would become New Mexico and southern Colorado. About seven thousand lived in California and another four thousand in Texas. Even fewer lived in Arizona.

Mass emigration from Mexico didn't begin until the first decades of the twentieth century. The migration was triggered in part by the Mexican Revolution (1910–1917) and facilitated by the construction of north-south railway lines. Labor shortages in the Southwest at the time, caused by government crackdowns on Asian immigrants, also attracted Mexicans. Railroad, mining, agriculture, and construction workers were needed to get the natural resources of the West to markets back East. And so, between 1900 and

1920 more than a quarter-million Mexican *enganchadores*, or laborers, headed north. Private labor contractors recruited them. Uncle Sam looked the other way. As the sociologists Douglas Massey, Jorge Durand, and Nolan Malone explain in *Beyond Smoke and Mirrors*, it would mark the beginning of America's schizophrenic relationship with Mexican immigrants.

The outbreak of WWI halted European immigration but induced a huge expansion of U.S. industries. This forced industrialists in Chicago, Kansas City, Los Angeles, and other cities facing labor shortages to rely even more heavily on foreign labor. Soon enough, Uncle Sam got in on the act. When Congress moved to restrict immigration in 1917 by imposing a head tax, literacy test, and other provisions on all new arrivals, the U.S. attorney general exempted Mexicans. And once the United States entered the war, write the authors, "the government assumed a direct role in labor recruitment by creating its own [foreign] worker recruitment program."

Throughout the 1920s, when Congress was closing off immigration from Europe, the established quotas never included Mexicans, or any other countries in the western hemisphere. "Although the total number of immigrants was capped at 357,000 in 1921, then lowered to 164,000 in 1924 and 154,000 in 1929," write the authors, "these numerical limitations were never applied to Mexico, whose nationals were free to enter without quantitative restrictions and did so in large numbers." It wasn't until the Great Depression that public sentiment turned against Mexican immigrants.

Policy makers and assorted demagogues in the press found in the Latino migrants a convenient scapegoat for high unemployment. Like today, Mexicans were accused of simultaneously stealing jobs and living on the dole. Deportation campaigns followed, and between 1930 and 1940 the Mexican population in the United States fell by more than 40 percent.

But the 1940s brought another world war, another economic boom, another acute labor shortage, and finally, another government program to recruit Mexican workers. This time, they were called braceros, and some 5 million entered the country during the program's twenty-two-year history. "Although originally envisioned as a temporary wartime measure," write Massey, Durand, and Malone, "the booming postwar economy perpetuated growers' fears of a labor shortage, and under considerable pressure from the Texas and California delegations, Congress extended the bracero program on a year-to-year basis through the late 1940s."

In 1951 they made it permanent, and it stayed that way for thirteen years. Anti-immigrant sentiment grew during the Korean War and the McCarthy era, culminating with the deportation of 1.2 million illegal immigrants during Operation Wetback in 1954. But even this temporary crackdown was paired with an expansion of legal immigration. And by the time pressure from U.S. labor unions ended the Bracero Program a decade later, illegal immigration from Mexico had been all but eliminated.

Even after the program's termination, however, U.S. policy sent mixed signals to both employers and migrants. Employers could hire undocumented workers with impunity, and so the availability of jobs continued to serve as a magnet. From 1965 to 1986, nothing in U.S. labor law stopped businesses from employing illegal aliens. "In fact," notes Dan Griswold of the Cato Institute, "under the 'Texas Proviso' inserted into the 1952 Immigration and Nationality Act at the behest of the Texas delegation, authorities were explicitly prohibited from prosecuting employers for hiring them. Thus, millions of Mexicans were able to enter the United States during this period and work for U.S. companies and farmers without significant fear of government interference." In effect, a de facto guest-worker program had replaced the Bracero policy. Restrictionists like to blame the 1965 repeal of immigration quotas for today's influx of Mexicans, but those quotas never applied to Mexico. It was the 1965 law that put in place quotas on Mexico and other countries in the western hemisphere for the first time. And it launched a new era of illegal immigration from Latin America. In the 1970s alone border apprehensions rose five-fold.

HOMELAND SECURITY

At least since the mid-1980s, restrictionist policies have reigned supreme. The federal government has steadily invested more money and effort to stop illegal immigration through various enforcement measures. Ed Meese, Alan Simpson, and other leading opponents of immigration at the time, heralded the 1986 Immigration Control and Reform Act (ICRA). They demanded sanctions for employers who knowingly hired illegal aliens, and ICRA provided them, along with a new false-document industry that continues to grow.

In 1994, the North American Free Trade Agreement (NAFTA) took effect. But even as we liberated the cross-border flows of capital, goods, and services, we persisted in trying to stop the free movement of people. At the urging of Texas Congressman Lamar Smith, among others, the 1990s saw a tripling of the border patrol. In addition, the Clinton administration initiated Operation Hold the Line, Operation Blockade, and Operation Gatekeeper, which involved planting patrols, three-tier fences, remote-control cameras and motion-detection devices along the more popular corridors for illegals, such as El Paso and San Diego. It didn't work. For all our troubles, illegal immigration still rose by 5.5 million people between 1990 and 2000.

To this day, we continue emphasizing enforcement above all else. By 2002, the border patrol's budget was $1.6 billion, a ten-fold increase over 1986. Over the same period the number of hours spent patrolling the border grew by a factor of eight. Meanwhile, between 480,000 and 660,000 illegal immigrants were entering the United States each year.

When President Bush took office in 2001, we had about 9,000 border patrol officers. The number increased by 50 percent to 13,500 in 2007, and the administration aims to double it by the end of Bush's term. Bush's 2008 budget called for spending $13 billion to strengthen border security and immigration enforcement. That includes $1 billion to build fences and virtual barriers. Since 2001, Congress has increased funding for border security by 145 percent. "We will have 370 miles of fence built by the end of 2008," Michael Chertoff told me. "We're also developing the first stage of what will ultimately be an across-the-border virtual technology fence, and in the interim we've had the border patrol augmented by the National Guard."

In 2005, Congress even flirted with the idea of making illegal immigration a felony, though eventually decided against it. Representative James Sensenbrenner led the effort. He wanted all 12 million illegal aliens in the country recategorized as felons, which would disqualify them from ever gaining legal status and automatically make them deportable. Then someone reminded Sensenbrenner that these wouldn't be simple deportation hearings. People in the United States who have been charged with a criminal offense are entitled to a lawyer and a day in court. Learning of these complications, Sensenbrenner backed off.

Many people mistakenly believed that being in the country illegally is already a criminal act. It is not and never has been. It's a civil violation, like a traffic infraction. Being here without authorization is certainly against the law, but it's a civil offense, not a criminal one. As the Congressional Research Service report "Immigration Enforcement Within the United States" put it in 2006: "Being illegally present in the U.S. has always been a civil, not criminal, violation of the [Immigration and Nationality Act], and subsequent deportation and associated administrative processes are civil proceedings."

Glenn Beck, a radio talk show host with a Sensenbrenner-type grasp of immigration law, was apparently unaware of this fact when he invited presidential hopeful Rudy Giuliani on his show in the summer of 2007. The following exchange ensued:

> BECK: [I]isn't illegal immigration a crime in and of itself?
>
> GIULIANI: No . . .
>
> BECK: You're protecting criminals by saying that being treated as a criminal is unfair.
>
> GIULIANI: Glenn, it's not a crime. I know that's very hard for people to understand, but it's not a federal crime. . . . I was U.S. attorney in the southern district of New York. So believe me, I know this. In fact, when you throw an immigrant out of the country, it's not a criminal proceeding. It's a civil proceeding.
>
> BECK: Is it—
>
> GIULIANI: One of the things that Congress wanted to do a year ago is to make it a crime, which indicates that it isn't.
>
> BECK: Should it be?
>
> GIULIANI: Should it be? No, it shouldn't be, because the

government wouldn't be able to prosecute it. We couldn't prosecute 12 million people. We have only 2 million people in jail right now for all the crimes that are committed in the country, 2.5 million. If you were to make it a crime, you would have to take the resources of the criminal justice system and increase it by about six. In other words, you'd have to take all the 800,000 police, and who knows how many police we would have to have.

BECK: So what's your solution?

GIULIANI: My solution is close the border to illegal immigration.

Similar to Michael Chertoff and Tom Ridge, Giuliani believes state and local police departments have more important things to do than chase down economic migrants. And his record of economic growth and reducing crime in New York—it became America's safest large city on his watch, notwithstanding the presence of some 400,000 illegal aliens—suggests that Giuliani had his priorities straight.

Our maniacal focus on enforcement has failed to stop illegal immigration, but there have been unintended consequences aplenty. Increasing patrols in California and Texas has resulted in more crossings in Arizona and other regions, where mountains and desert have claimed at least 4,500 lives since 1994. The aforementioned document-fraud industry is booming, and human smuggling fees have skyrocketed. Traditional circular migration, whereby foreign workers come for the growing season and return home afterward, is less common because the trip has become more treacherous. Now migrants stay year-round and seek out work to sustain them after the harvest. They've gradually moved into other industries, such as construction, hospitality, and health care. Today, just 4 percent of illegal immigrants work in farming, and growers face regular labor shortages.

We're also wasting a lot of money. To appreciate how much, consider this observation from Gordon Hanson, an economist at the University of California at San Diego:

> For the sake of argument, take literally the estimate that illegal immigration was costing the economy the equivalent of 0.07 percent of GDP annually as of 2002. In that year, the Immigration and Naturalization Service spent $4.2 billion (or 0.04 percent of GDP) on border and interior enforcement, including the detention and removal of illegal aliens, in a year in which half a million net new illegal immigrants entered the country. The $13 billion in proposed border security spending for next year [2008] is already two-and-a half times that figure at 0.10 percent of GDP.

In other words, the amount of money we spend to keep illegal immigrants out of the country now exceeds the amount of economic "damage" they supposedly cause. Remember that the next time you're told that we need to spend more money to beef up the border.

Reasonable people agree that illegal immigration should be reduced. The question isn't whether it's a problem but how to solve it. Historically, the best results have come from providing more legal ways for immigrants to enter the country. Most of these people are not predisposed to crime or terrorists in waiting. They are economic migrants who would gladly use the front door if it were open to them. Post 9/11, knowing who's in the country has rightly taken on an urgency. But painting Latino immigrants as violent criminals or Islamofascists won't make us any safer. Nor will enforcing bad laws and polices, as opposed to reforming them. On the whole, immigrants are an asset to America, not a liability. We benefit from the labor, they benefit from the jobs. Our laws should acknowledge and reflect this reality, not deny it.

Let them in.

CONCLUSION

─────────────── ★ ───────────────

As I wrap up this book, the 2008 presidential primary season is just beginning. Immigration has figured prominently in the debates so far, particularly on the GOP side. Mitt Romney, Rudy Giuliani, Fred Thompson, and Mike Huckabee are all running as heirs to Reagan Republicanism. Yet they've fallen over each other in condemnation of President Bush's attempts to follow the Gipper's lead on immigration reform. Makes you wonder.

No self-respecting free-market adherent would ever dream of supporting laws that interrupt the free movement of goods and services across borders. But when it comes to laws that hamper the free movement of workers who produce those goods and services, too many conservatives today abandon their classical liberal principles. Adam Smith, J. C. L. Sismondi, David Ricardo, and John Stuart Mill give way to . . . Pat Buchanan. Some of us find this troubling.

Among Democrats, there's been much less restrictionist rhetoric, and not just because the political left tends to favor more liberal immigration policies. Strategically, the Democratic candidates have reasoned that it's best to sit on the sidelines and let Republicans fight among themselves. Nevertheless, Hillary Clinton stumbled when she got careless and appeared to endorse a proposal by New York Governor Eliot Spitzer to give driver's licenses to illegal aliens. The governor and the senator had logic on their side, to be sure. If we are not going to deport 12 million illegal immigrants—and we're not—it makes little sense, public policy-wise, to let them stay but not drive legally.

Some will drive anyway, which means more unlicensed and uninsured drivers on the road. But denying licenses to illegals is also counterproductive from a law enforcement and homeland security standpoint. Which is why people like William Bratton, the former police commissioner of New York and current chief of police in Los Angeles—and a man no one would accuse of being soft on crime or terrorism—supported the Spitzer plan. As Margaret Stock, who teaches national security law at the United States Military Academy at West Point, has noted, the collective Department of Motor Vehicle databases are the largest and most comprehensive law enforcement databases in the country. In a post-9/11 world, when knowing who's in the United States has never been more important, how does excluding 12 million residents from the nation's largest security database make us safer?

Nevertheless, public outcry, much of it facilitated by Lou Dobbs, forced Clinton to back off and led Spitzer to shelve his proposal. As we've seen in the preceding chapters, it's not uncommon for logic and reason to be crowded out of our emotionally charged national conversation about immigrants. At such times, we count on our elected leaders to have the courage of their convictions, even when it's unpopular. *Especially* when it's unpopular. The driver's license brouhaha revealed that when it comes to immigration reform, Senator Clinton and Governor Spitzer lack either courage or conviction. It also revealed that the GOP isn't the only party struggling with the issue. A Democrat in the White House won't automatically (or necessarily) fare any better on immigration reform than a Republican.

My primary goal in writing this book was to offer a rebuttal to some of the more common anti-immigrant arguments that I've come across while covering the issue as a *Wall Street Journal* editorialist. The received wisdom, courtesy of ratings-driven populists on talk radio and cable news outlets primarily, holds that immigrants cause more trouble than they're worth. We're constantly told that foreign-born workers are displacing native workers, that they're crippling our welfare-state apparatus, that they're criminally inclined, and that they aren't assimilating. Yet time and again, my own reporting and research found these claims to be overblown when they weren't counterfactual.

Economists across the political spectrum, from liberals like David Card to conservatives like Richard Vedder, have demonstrated that the free movement of labor adds efficiency and productivity to our economy. Hence, immigrants tend to stimulate economic growth rather than cause unemployment. Those conclusions are not cherry-picked exceptions. They are the rule. Indeed, the current economic literature is replete with such findings from, among many others, Pia Orrenius, Julian Simon, Gordon Hanson, John Whalley, Giovanni Peri, Bjorn Letnes, Jonathon Moses, David Henderson, Alberto Alesina, Tyler Cowen, Bob Hamilton, Jagdish Bhagwati, Philippe Legrain, and Grancesco Giavazzi.

Yes, you occasionally will come across a serious economist like George Borjas who makes the opposite argument. But even his research simply concludes that, at most, low-skill immigrants from Mexico might have a slight negative impact on this country's small (and shrinking) unskilled native labor force. It's also clear that on balance, Borjas is the outlier. If your anti-immigrant arguments are overly reliant on research like his, *you're* the one who's cherry picking. My intent in citing study upon economic study to make this point is not to bore the reader but rather to illustrate the vast gulf between populist bombast and mainstream eco-nomic thinking.

And so it goes with other oft-repeated contentions about immigrants and welfare, immigrants and crime, immigrants and assimilation—none of which hold up very well to scru-tiny. It turns out that the low-income immigrants who qual-ify for public benefits sign up at much lower rates than low-income natives. It turns out that immigrants also com-mit crimes at disproportionately lower rates than natives. And it turns out that the children of Latino immigrants are, in fact, learning English. What's more, they're learning it with the encouragement of their parents and despite the best efforts of bilingual education advocates and other net-tlesome multiculturalists.

Another goal of this book was to put today's debate into perspective. Scapegoating foreigners for domestic problems real or imagined is something of an American tradition. Any student of history knows that the complaints and criticisms lodged against today's Latinos were thrown at previous im-migrant groups. But how easily some of us forget.

Ireland was the source country of the first mass migra-tion to the United States. The Irish flooded America in the middle of the nineteenth century, particularly the cities. In 1850, more than a quarter of New York City's residents were born in Ireland. Throughout the 1800s, the United States absorbed Irish newcomers at more than double the rate of current Mexican immigration.

These Irish immigrants were dirt-poor peasants back home, but in America they settled in urban ghettos among their own kind, where crime and violence and disease were not uncommon. Most were uneducated. Many spoke no English. They worked as domestic servants, ditch diggers, stevedores, and in other low-skill, labor-intensive jobs that the natives shunned. They were stereotyped as slow-witted drunks and ne'er-do-wells who would never acculturate to America. They were considered members of an inferior race. Political cartoonists drew them with distinctly simian features. Restrictionists of the period called for rounding them up and shipping them back to their homeland before they destroyed our culture and social mores with their backward ways.

Of course, the naysayers were wrong. The Irish did assimilate. And then some. They produced writers, painters, and presidents. They produced doctors and lawyers and school teachers. They produced civic leaders and businessmen, including Henry Ford, whose father fled the Irish potato famine and who would go on to revolutionize transportation in America. According to the latest census figures, as of 2006, 31 percent of Irish Americans had at least a bachelor's degree, versus 27 percent of the nation as a whole. And the median annual income for households headed by an Irish American was $54,000, versus $48,000 for all households. Apparently, the children and grandchildren and great-grandchildren of all those hard-working Irish immigrants turned out okay. And although the Irish experience has been replicated by other large immigrant groups from Europe and Asia, this history is often ignored or played down when we discuss Latino immigration today. The opposite should be the case.

People often say that they support legal immigration and oppose illegal immigration. But saying that you oppose unlawful behavior isn't really saying much. All reasonable people oppose illegal behavior in principle. The issue with respect to immigration is whether our current laws make sense, whether they're accomplishing the intended goals of the policy makers who put them in place. Bad laws need to be reformed, not enforced, and current immigration law has left us with upward of 12 million illegal immigrants in the United States. Is two-tier fencing, a militarized border, and stricter internal enforcement of current law feasible, politically or otherwise? Would it make us safer? What would it do to our traditions? What would it do to our economy? How would it impact the cost of food, housing, and countless other goods and services? Would it put U.S. companies at a competitive disadvantage in the global marketplace? Would it result in more offshoring and outsourcing of jobs?

Although it will surely be characterized as such, this book is not an argument for erasing America's borders or dissolving our nation-state. Nor do I pretend that immigration has no economic costs. It does have costs, particularly in border regions and states with generous public benefits. But when those costs are properly weighed against the gains, open immigration and liberal trade policies still make more sense than protectionism, from both a security and an economic standpoint. The United States needs to better regulate cross-border labor flows, not end them. We still have much more to gain than lose from people who come here to seek a better life.

SELECT BIBLIOGRAPHY

───────────────── ★ ─────────────────

Alesina, Alberto, and Francesco Giavazzi. *The Future of Europe: Reform or Decline.* MIT Press, 2006.

Anderson, Terry L., ed. *You Have to Admit It's Getting Better: From Economic Prosperity to Environmental Quality.* Hoover Institution Press, 2004.

Bailey, Ronald, ed., and Competitive Enterprise Institute. *Global Warming and Other Eco-Myths: How the Environmental Movement Uses False Science to Scare Us to Death.* Prima Publishing, 2002.

Barone, Michael. *Our Country: The Shaping of America from Roosevelt to Reagan.* Free Press, 1990.

———. *The New Americans: How the Melting Pot Can Work Again.* Regnery, 2001.

Bauer, P. T. *Equality, the Third World, and Economic Delusion.* Harvard University Press, 1981.

Bean, Frank D., and Gillian Stevens. *America's Newcomers and the Dynamics of Diversity.* Russell Sage Foundation, 2003.

Becker, Gary S., and Guity Nashat Becker. *The Economics of Life: From Baseball to Affirmative Action to Immigration, How Real-World Issues Affect Our Everyday Life.* McGraw-Hill, 1997.

Bickel, Alexander M. *The Morality of Consent.* Yale University Press, 1975.

Borjas, George J. *Heaven's Door: Immigration Policy and the American Economy.* Princeton University Press, 1999.

Buchholz, Todd G. *Bringing the Jobs Home: How the Left Created the Outsourcing Crisis—and How We Can Fix It.* Sentinel, 2004.

Caplan, Bryan. *The Myth of the Rational Voter: Why Democracies Choose Bad Policies.* Princeton University Press, 2007.

Chavez, Linda. *Out of the Barrio: Toward a New Politics of Hispanic Assimilation.* Basic Books, 1991.

Cowen, Tyler. *Creative Destruction: How Globalization Is Changing the World's Cultures.* Princeton University Press, 2002.

Daniels, Roger. *Coming to America: A History of Immigration and Ethnicity in American Life.* 2nd ed. Perennial, 2002.

———. *Guarding the Golden Door.* Hill and Wang, 2004.

Friedman, Milton. *Capitalism and Freedom.* University of Chicago Press, 1962.

Gilder, George. *Wealth and Poverty.* Basic Books, 1981.

Goldie, Mark, ed. *Locke: Political Essays.* Cambridge University Press, 1997.

Hanson, Victor Davis. *Mexifornia: A State of Becoming.* Encounter Books, 2003.

Hazlitt, Henry. *Economics in One Lesson.* Crown, 1946.

Huber, Peter. *Hard Green: Saving the Environment from the Environmentalists.* Basic Books, 1999.

Huntington, Samuel P. *Who Are We: The Challenges to America's National Identity.* Simon and Schuster, 2004.

Jacoby, Tamar, ed. *Reinventing the Melting Pot: The New Immigrants and What It Means to Be an American.* Basic Books, 2004.

LeMay, Michael C. *Guarding the Gates: Immigration and National Security.* Praeger Security International, 2006.

Lomborg, Bjorn. *The Skeptical Environmentalist: Measuring the Real State of the World.* Cambridge University Press, 2001.

Massey, Douglas S., Jorge Durand, and Nolan J. Malone. *Beyond Smoke and Mirrors: Mexican Immigration in an Era of Economic Integration.* Russell Sage Foundation, 2002.

Myers, Dowell. *Immigrants and Boomers: Forging a New Social Contract for the Future of America.* Russell Sage Foundation, 2007.

Perlmann, Joel. *Italians Then, Mexicans Now: Immigrant Origins and Second-Generation Progress, 1890 to 2000.* Russell Sage Foundation, 2005.

Salins, Peter D. *Assimilation, American Style.* Basic Books, 1997.

Simon, Julian L. *The Economics of Population Growth.* Princeton University Press, 1977.

———. *The Economic Consequences of Immigration.* 2nd ed. University of Michigan Press, 1999.

Simon, Julian L., ed. *The Economics of Population: Classical Writings.* Transaction Publishers, 1998.

Smith, James P., and Barry Edmonston, eds. *The New Americans: Economic, Demographic, and Fiscal Effects of Immigration.* National Academy Press, 1997.

Sowell, Thomas. *Migrations and Cultures: A World View.* Basic Books, 1996.

————. *On Classical Economics.* Yale University Press, 2006.

Wattenberg, Ben J. *Fewer: How the New Demography of Depopulation Will Shape Our Future.* Ivan R. Dee, 2004.

Wolfe, Alan. *One Nation, After All: What Middle-Class Americans Really Think About God, Country, Family, Racism, Welfare, Immigration, Homosexuality, Work, the Right, the Left and Each Other.* Viking, 1998.

Zolberg, Aristide R. *A Nation By Design: Immigration Policy in the Fashioning of America.* Russell Sage Foundation, 2006.

ACKNOWLEDGMENTS

★

Naomi Schaefer Riley, my wife and *Wall Street Journal* colleague, came up with the idea for this book and spent many hours reading over and critiquing the manuscript. More important, Naomi created a home environment conducive to writing, which was no mean feat given that she gave birth to our first child within days of my signing the book contract. I thank her.

My other colleagues on *The Wall Street Journal* editorial page have also provided invaluable intellectual guidance and stimulation. I can't overstate the satisfaction that derives from being part of a staff of professional journalists who put truth above popularity. A special thanks goes to Paul Gigot,

Dan Henninger, and Melanie Kirkpatrick, whom I've had the pleasure to work with for the past fourteen years. I'd also like to thank John Fund and Steve Moore for being so selfless with sources and contacts.

A fuller understanding of migration and its consequences requires some familiarity with multiple disciplines, including economics, demography, sociology, statistics, political science, history, national security, and law. To that end, I'd like to thank the following individuals, all of whom were interviewed for this book and whose expertise informed my conclusions: Richard Alba, Michael Chertoff, Nicholas Eberstadt, Ross Emmett, Walter Ewing, Michael Fix, Diana Furchtgott-Roth, Daniel Griswold, Ron Haskins, Steven Hayward, Kay Hymowitz, Daniel Mitchell, Dowell Myers, Seth Norton, Michael O'Hanlon, Pia Orrenius, Jeffrey Passel, Giovanni Peri, Tom Ridge, Simon Rosenberg, Peter Salins, Bernd Schwieren, Jeremy Shapiro, and Richard Vedder.

Stuart Anderson has spent countless hours explaining (and re-explaining) the intricacies of U.S. immigration law to me, and he's always done it with grace and good humor. Veteran opinion journalists Fred Barnes, Michael Barone, Linda Chavez, Tamar Jacoby, and Michael Medved also have been very generous with their time.

A final note of thanks goes to my editors Brett Valley and Patrick Mulligan at at Gotham; and to my agent, Emma Parry, whose hard bargaining and gentle hand-holding brought this book to fruition.

INDEX

★

assimilation (*continued*)
distance traveled by Mexican
immigrants and, 141–42
educational attainment and,
143, 144, 149–51
English use and, 143–45
European immigrants and,
129, 134, 138–41,
147–48
exaggeration of permanence
of immigration and,
142–43
homeownership and, 143,
145–46
illusion of nonadvancement
and, 143–44
income gap and, 147–48
multiculturalist elites and,
155–57
poverty and, 143, 145, 146
racism and, 128–35
U.S. assimilation model and,
152–54, 157
attrition approach to reducing
illegal immigration,
204–5
automation delay argument,
75–77

Barnes, Fred, 177–78
Barone, Michael, 140, 142–44,
171–73
Barry, Marion, 172
Beach, William, 116–17
Beauprez, Bob, 166
Beck, Glenn, 176, 213–14
Beck, Roy, 15, 20, 24
Becker, Gary, 38

Bennett, Bill, 43, 176
*Betrayal: How Union Bosses Shake
Down Their Members and
Corrupt American Politics*
(Chavez), 127
Beyond Smoke and Mirrors
(Massey et al), 208
Beyond the Melting Pot (Moyni-
han), 172
Bhagwati, Jagdish, 220
Bierce, Ambrose, 9
blacks
Bush Administration ad-
dresses in 2005 and 2006,
167
economic advancement, 53,
61–62, 80–88
labor participation rate, 120–
21, 151
political party identification,
170–72
teen pregnancy, 151
Bloom, Allan, 155
Blunt, Roy, 162
Boas, Franz, 29
Booker, Corey, 191–92
border security, 7, 197–206,
211–12
Borjas, George, 77–79, 103, 114,
220
Bottomless Well, The (Huber and
Mills), 38
Bracero Program, 76, 184–85, 209
Bratton, William, 218
Brimelow, Peter, 23, 130, 131
Brown, Lester, 33
Buchanan, Pat, 4, 5, 21, 53, 137–38,
188, 189, 201, 218

ORLAND PARK
PUBLIC LIBRARY
A Natural Connection

14921 Ravinia Avenue
Orland Park, IL 60462

708-428-5100
orlandparklibrary.org